TOUCHSTONE

MICHAEL MCCARTHY
JEANNE MCCARTEN
HELEN SANDIFORD

STUDENT'S BOOK

CAMBRIDGE
UNIVERSITY PRESS

CAMBRIDGE UNIVERSITY PRESS
Cambridge, New York, Melbourne, Madrid, Cape Town, Singapore, São Paulo

Cambridge University Press
40 West 20th Street, New York, NY 10011-4211, USA

www.cambridge.org
Information on this title: www.cambridge.org/9780521666053

First published 2005
2nd printing

Printed in Hong Kong, China

A catalog record for this publication is available from the British Library

ISBN-13   978-0-521-66605-3 pack consisting of student's book and self-study audio CD/CD-ROM (Windows®, Mac®)
ISBN-10   0-521-66605-8 pack consisting of student's book and self-study audio CD/CD-ROM (Windows®, Mac®)

ISBN-13   978-0-521-60134-4 pack consisting of student's book/Korea and self-study audio CD/CD-ROM (Windows®, Mac®)
ISBN-10   0-521-60134-7 pack consisting of student's book/Korea and self-study audio CD/CD-ROM (Windows®, Mac®)

ISBN-13   978-0-521-60135-1 pack consisting of student's book A and self-study audio CD/CD-ROM (Windows®, Mac®)
ISBN-10   0-521-60135-5 pack consisting of student's book A and self-study audio CD/CD-ROM (Windows®, Mac®)

ISBN-13   978-0-521-60136-8 pack consisting of student's book B and self-study audio CD/CD-ROM (Windows®, Mac®)
ISBN-10   0-521-60136-3 pack consisting of student's book B and self-study audio CD/CD-ROM (Windows®, Mac®)

ISBN-13   978-0-521-66604-6 workbook
ISBN-10   0-521-66604-X workbook

ISBN-13   978-0-521-60137-5 workbook A
ISBN-10   0-521-60137-1 workbook A

ISBN-13   978-0-521-60138-2 workbook B
ISBN-10   0-521-60138-X workbook B

ISBN-13   978-0-521-66603-9 teacher's edition
ISBN-10   0-521-66603-1 teacher's edition

ISBN-13   978-0-521-66600-8 CDs (audio)
ISBN-10   0-521-66600-7 CDs (audio)

ISBN-13   978-0-521-66601-5 cassettes
ISBN-10   0-521-66601-5 cassettes

Art direction, book design, photo research, and layout services: Adventure House, NYC
Audio production: Full House, NYC

Authors' acknowledgments

Touchstone has benefited from extensive development research. The authors and publishers would like to extend their particular thanks to the following reviewers, consultants, and piloters for their valuable insights and suggestions.

Reviewers and consultants:

Thomas Job Lane and Marilia de M. Zanella from **Associação Alumni**, São Paulo, Brazil; Simon Banha from **Phil Young's English School**, Curitiba, Brazil; Katy Cox from **Casa Thomas Jefferson**, Brasilia, Brazil; Rodrigo Santana from **CCBEU**, Goiânia, Brazil; Cristina Asperti, Nancy H. Lake, and Airton Pretini Junior from **CEL LEP**, São Paulo, Brazil; Sonia Cury from **Centro Britânico**, São Paulo, Brazil; Daniela Alves Meyer from **IBEU**, Rio de Janeiro, Brazil; Ayeska Farias from **Mai English**, Belo Horizonte, Brazil; Solange Cassiolato from **LTC**, São Paulo, Brazil; Fernando Prestes Maia from **Polidiomas**, São Paulo, Brazil; Chris Ritchie and Debora Schisler from **Seven Idiomas**, São Paulo, Brazil; Maria Teresa Maiztegui and Joacyr de Oliveira from **União Cultural EEUU**, São Paulo, Brazil; Sakae Onoda from **Chiba University of Commerce**, Ichikawa, Japan; James Boyd and Ann Conlon from **ECC Foreign Language Institute**, Osaka, Japan; Catherine Chamier from **ELEC**, Tokyo, Japan; Janaka Williams, Japan; David Aline from **Kanagawa University**, Yokohama, Japan; Brian Long from **Kyoto University of Foreign Studies**, Kyoto, Japan; Alistair Home and Brian Quinn from **Kyushu University**, Fukuoka, Japan; Rafael Dovale from **Matsushita Electric Industrial Co., Ltd.**, Osaka, Japan; Bill Acton, Michael Herriman, Bruce Monk, and Alan Thomson from **Nagoya University of Commerce**, Nisshin, Japan; Alan Bessette from **Poole Gakuin University**, Osaka, Japan; Brian Collins from **Sundai Foreign Language Institute, Tokyo College of Music**, Tokyo, Japan; Todd Odgers from **The Tokyo Center for Language and Culture**, Tokyo, Japan; Jion Hanagata from **Tokyo Foreign Language College**, Tokyo, Japan; Peter Collins and Charlene Mills from **Tokai University**, Hiratsuka, Japan; David Stewart from **Tokyo Institute of Technology**, Tokyo, Japan; Alberto Peto Villalobos from **Cenlex Santo Tomás**, Mexico City, Mexico; Diana Jones and Carlos Lizarraga from **Instituto Angloamericano**, Mexico City, Mexico; Raúl Mar and María Teresa Monroy from **Universidad de Cuautitlán Izcalli**, Mexico City, Mexico; JoAnn Miller from **Universidad del Valle de México**, Mexico City, Mexico; Orlando Carranza from **ICPNA**, Peru; Sister Melanie Bair and Jihyeon Jeon from **The Catholic University of Korea**, Seoul, South Korea; Peter E. Nelson from **Chung-Ang University**, Seoul, South Korea; Joseph Schouweiler from **Dongguk University**, Seoul, South Korea; Michael Brazil and Sean Witty from **Gwangwoon University**, Seoul, South Korea; Kelly Martin and Larry Michienzi from **Hankook FLS University**, Seoul, South Korea; Scott Duerstock and Jane Miller from **Konkuk University**, Seoul, South Korea; Athena Pichay from **Korea University**, Seoul, South Korea; Lane Darnell Bahl, Susan Caesar, and Aaron Hughes from **Korea University**, Seoul, South Korea; Farzana Hyland and Stephen van Vlack from **Sookmyung Women's University**, Seoul, South Korea; Hae-Young Kim, Terry Nelson, and Ron Schafrick from **Sungkyunkwan University**, Seoul, South Korea; Mary Chen and Michelle S. M. Fan from **Chinese Cultural University**, Taipei, Taiwan; Joseph Sorell from **Christ's College**, Taipei, Taiwan; Dan Aldridge and Brian Kleinsmith from **ELSI**, Taipei, Taiwan; Ching-Shyang Anna Chien and Duen-Yeh Charles Chang from **Hsin Wu Institute of Technology**, Taipei, Taiwan; Timothy Hogan, Andrew Rooney, and Dawn Young from **Language Training and Testing Center**, Taipei, Taiwan; Jen Mei Hsu and Yu-hwei Eunice Shih from **National Taiwan Normal University**, Taipei, Taiwan; Roma Starczewska and Su-Wei Wang from **PQ3R Taipei Language and Computer Center**, Taipei, Taiwan; Elaine Paris from **Shih Chien University**, Taipei, Taiwan; Jennifer Castello from **Cañada College**, Redwood City, California, USA; Dennis Johnson, Gregory Keech, and Penny Larson from **City College of San Francisco – Institute for International Students**, San Francisco, California, USA; Ditra Henry from **College of Lake County**, Gray's Lake, Illinois, USA; Madeleine Murphy from **College of San Mateo**, San Mateo, California, USA; Ben Yoder from **Harper College**, Palatine, Illinois, USA; Christine Aguila, John Lanier, Armando Mata, and Ellen Sellergren from **Lakeview Learning Center**, Chicago, Illinois, USA; Ellen Gomez from **Laney College**, Oakland, California, USA; Brian White from **Northeastern Illinois University**, Chicago, Illinois, USA; Randi Reppen from **Northern Arizona University**, Flagstaff, Arizona, USA; Janine Gluud from **San Francisco State University – College of Extended Learning**, San Francisco, California, USA; Peg Sarosy from **San Francisco State University – American Language Institute**, San Francisco, California, USA; David Mitchell from **UC Berkley Extension, ELP – English Language Program**, San Francisco, California, USA; Eileen Censotti, Kim Knutson, Dave Onufrock, Marnie Ramker, and Jerry Stanfield from **University of Illinois at Chicago – Tutorium in Intensive English**, Chicago, Illinois, USA; Johnnie Johnson Hafernik from **University of San Francisco, ESL Program**, San Francisco, California, USA; Judy Friedman from **New York Institute of Technology**, New York, New York, USA; Sheila Hackner from **St. John's University**, New York, New York, USA; Joan Lesikin from **William Paterson University**, Wayne, New Jersey, USA; Linda Pelc from **LaGuardia Community College**, Long Island City, New York, USA; Tamara Plotnick from **Pace University**, New York, USA; Lenore Rosenbluth from **Montclair State University**, Montclair, New Jersey, USA; Suzanne Seidel from **Nassau Community College**, Garden City, New York, USA; Debbie Un from **New York University, New School**, and **LaGuardia Community College**, New York, New York, USA; Cynthia Wiseman from **Hunter College**, New York, New York, USA; Aaron Lawson from **Cornell University**, Ithaca, New York, USA, for his help in corpus research; Belkis Yanes from **CTC Belo Monte**, Caracas, Venezuela; Victoria García from **English World**, Caracas, Venezuela; Kevin Bandy from **LT Language Teaching Services**, Caracas, Venezuela; Ivonne Quintero from **PDVSA**, Caracas, Venezuela.

Piloters:

Daniela Jorge from **ELFE Idiomas**, São Paulo, Brazil; Eloisa Marchesi Oliveira from **ETE Professor Camargo Aranha**, São Paulo, Brazil; Marilena Wanderley Pessoa from **IBEU**, Rio de Janeiro, Brazil; Marcia Lotaif from **LTC**, São Paulo, Brazil; Mirlei Valenzi from **USP English on Campus**, São Paulo, Brazil; Jelena Johanovic from **YEP International**, São Paulo, Brazil; James Steinman from **Osaka International College for Women**, Moriguchi, Japan; Brad Visgatis from **Osaka International University for Women**, Moriguchi, Japan; William Figoni from **Osaka Institute of Technology**, Osaka, Japan; Terry O'Brien from **Otani Women's University**, Tondabayashi, Japan; Gregory Kennerly from **YMCA Language Center** piloted at **Hankyu SHS**, Osaka, Japan; Daniel Alejandro Ramos and Salvador Enríquez Castaneda from **Instituto Cultural Mexicano-Norteamericano de Jalisco**, Guadalajara, Mexico; Patricia Robinson and Melida Valdes from **Universidad de Guadalajara**, Guadalajara, Mexico.

We would also like to thank the people who arranged recordings:

Debbie Berktold, Bobbie Gore, Bill Kohler, Aaron Lawson, Terri Massin, Traci Suiter, Bryan Swan, and the many people who agreed to be recorded.

The authors would also like to thank the **editorial** and **production** team:

Sue Aldcorn, Eleanor K. Barnes, Janet Battiste, Sylvia P. Bloch, David Bohlke, Karen Brock, Jeff Chen, Sylvia Dare, Karen Davy, Deborah Goldblatt, Paul Heacock, Louisa Hellegers, Cindee Howard, Eliza Jensen, Lesley Koustaff, Heather McCarron, Lise R. Minovitz, Diana Nam, Kathy Niemczyk, Sandra Pike, Bill Preston, Janet Raskin, Mary Sandre, Tamar Savir, Susannah Sodergren, Shelagh Speers, Kayo Taguchi, Mary Vaughn, Jennifer Wilkin, and all the design and production team at Adventure House.

And these Cambridge University Press **staff** and **advisors**:

Yumiko Akeba, Jim Anderson, Kanako Aoki, Mary Louise Baez, Carlos Barbisan, Alexandre Canizares, Cruz Castro, Kathleen Corley, Kate Cory-Wright, Riitta da Costa, Peter Davison, Elizabeth Fuzikava, Steven Golden, Yuri Hara, Catherine Higham, Gareth Knight, João Madureira, Andy Martin, Alejandro Martínez, Nigel McQuitty, Carine Mitchell, Mark O'Neil, Rebecca Ou, Antonio Puente, Colin Reublinger, Andrew Robinson, Dan Schulte, Kumiko Sekioka, Catherine Shih, Howard Siegelman, Ivan Sorrentino, Ian Sutherland, Alcione Tavares, Koen Van Landeghem, Sergio Varela, and Ellen Zlotnick.

In addition, the authors would like to thank Colin Hayes and Jeremy Mynott for making the project possible in the first place. Most of all, very special thanks are due to Mary Vaughn for her dedication, support, and professionalism. Helen Sandiford would like to thank her family and especially her husband, Bryan Swan, for his support and love.

Welcome to Touchstone!

We created the **Touchstone** series with the help of the *Cambridge International Corpus* of North American English. The corpus is a large database of language from everyday conversations, radio and television broadcasts, and newspapers and books.

Using computer software, we analyze the corpus to find out how people actually use English. We use the corpus as a "touchstone" to make sure that each lesson teaches you authentic and useful language. The corpus helps us choose and explain the grammar, vocabulary, and conversation strategies you need to communicate successfully in English.

Touchstone makes learning English fun. It gives you many different opportunities to interact with your classmates. You can exchange personal information, take class surveys, role-play situations, play games, and discuss topics of personal interest. Using **Touchstone**, you can develop confidence in your ability to understand real-life English and to express yourself clearly and effectively in everyday situations.

We hope you enjoy using **Touchstone** and wish you every success with your English classes.

Michael McCarthy
Jeanne McCarten
Helen Sandiford

Unit features

Getting started presents new grammar in natural contexts such as surveys, interviews, conversations, and phone messages.

Figure it out challenges you to notice how grammar works.

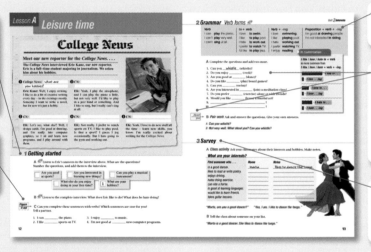

Grammar is presented in clear charts.

Grammar exercises give you practice with new structures and opportunities to exchange personal information with your classmates.

Survey encourages you to ask your classmates interesting questions.

Building vocabulary uses pictures to introduce new words and expressions.

Word sort helps you organize vocabulary and then use it to interact with your classmates.

Speaking naturally helps you understand and use natural pronunciation and intonation.

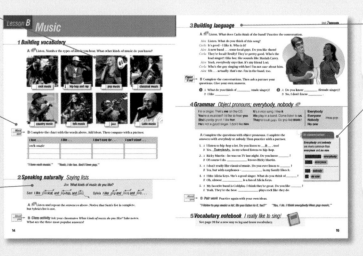

Building language builds on the grammar presented in Lesson A.

In conversation panels tell you about the grammar and vocabulary that are most frequent in spoken North American English.

iv

Conversation strategy helps you "manage" conversations better. In this lesson, you learn how to say **no** in a friendly way. The strategies are based on examples from the corpus.

Strategy plus teaches important expressions for conversation management, such as **really** and **not really**.

Listening and speaking skills are often practiced together. You listen to a variety of conversations based on real-life language. Tasks include "listen and react" activities.

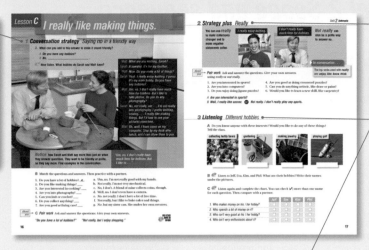

Reading has interesting texts from newspapers, magazines, and the Internet. The activities help you develop reading skills.

Writing tasks include e-mails, letters, short articles, and material for Web pages.

Help notes give you information on things like punctuation, linking ideas, and organizing information.

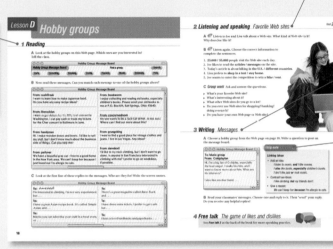

Vocabulary notebook is a page of fun activities to help you organize and write down vocabulary.

On your own is a practical task to help you learn vocabulary outside of class.

Fun facts from the corpus tell you the most frequent words and expressions for different topics.

Free talk helps you engage in free conversation with your classmates.

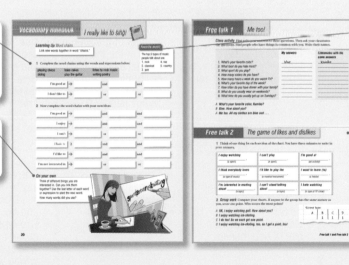

Other features

A **Touchstone checkpoint** after every three units reviews grammar, vocabulary, and conversation strategies.

A **Self-study Audio CD/ CD-ROM** gives you more practice with listening, speaking, and vocabulary building.

The **Class Audio Program** presents the conversations and listening activities in natural, lively English.

The **Workbook** gives you language practice and extra reading and writing activities. **Progress checks** help you assess your progress.

Touchstone *Level 2 Scope and sequence*

	Functions / Topics	Grammar	Vocabulary	Conversation strategies	Pronunciation
Unit 1 **Making friends** *pages 1–10*	• Ask questions to get to know your classmates • Talk about yourself, your family, and your favorite things • Show you have something in common	• Review of simple present and present of *be* in questions and statements • Responses with *too* and *either*	• Review of types of TV shows, clothes, food, and weekend activities	• Start a conversation with someone you don't know • Use *actually* to give or "correct" information	• Stress and intonation in questions and answers
Unit 2 **Interests** *pages 11–20*	• Ask about people's interests and hobbies • Talk about your interests, hobbies, and taste in music	• Verb forms after *can / can't, love, like,* etc., and prepositions • Object pronouns • *Everybody, everyone, nobody,* and *no one*	• Interests and hobbies • Types of music	• Say *no* in a friendly way • Use *really* and *not really* to make statements stronger or softer	• Saying lists
Unit 3 **Health** *pages 21–30*	• Talk about how to stay healthy • Describe common health problems • Talk about what you do when you have a health problem	• Simple present and present continuous • Joining clauses with *if* and *when*	• Ways to stay healthy • Common health problems • Common remedies	• Encourage people to say more to keep a conversation going • Show surprise	• Contrasts

Touchstone *checkpoint Units 1–3*   *pages 31–32*

	Functions / Topics	Grammar	Vocabulary	Conversation strategies	Pronunciation
Unit 4 **Celebrations** *pages 33–42*	• Talk about birthdays, celebrations, and favorite holidays • Describe how you celebrate special days • Talk about plans and predictions	• Future with *going to* • Indirect objects • Indirect object pronouns • Present continuous for the future	• Months of the year • Days of the month • Special days, celebrations, and holidays • Things people do to celebrate special days	• Use "vague" expressions like *and everything* • Give "vague" responses like *I don't know* and *Maybe* when you're not sure	• Reduction of *going to*
Unit 5 **Growing up** *pages 43–52*	• Talk about life events and memories of growing up • Talk about school and your teenage years	• Review of simple past in questions and statements • *be born* • General and specific use of determiners	• Time expressions for the past • Saying years • School subjects	• Correct things you say with expressions like *Well*; *Actually*; and *No, wait* • Use *I mean* to correct yourself when you say the wrong word or name	• Reduction of *did you*
Unit 6 **Around town** *pages 53–62*	• Ask and answer questions about places in a town • Give directions • Offer help and ask for directions • Talk about stores and favorite places in your town • Recommend places in your neighborhood	• *Is there?* and *Are there?* • Pronouns *one* and *some* • Offers and requests with *Can* and *Could*	• Places in town • Location expressions • Expressions for asking and giving directions	• Repeat key words to check information • Use "checking" expressions to check information • Use "echo" questions to check information	• Word stress in compound nouns

Touchstone *checkpoint Units 4–6*   *pages 63–64*

Listening	Reading	Writing	Vocabulary notebook	Free talk
What's the question? ▪ Listen to answers and match them with questions *Sally's party* ▪ Listen to responses and match them to conversation starters; then listen for more information	*How to improve your conversation skills* ▪ A magazine article giving advice	▪ Write an article giving advice on how to improve something ▪ Review of punctuation	*Webs of words* ▪ Use word webs to organize new vocabulary	*Me too!* ▪ Class activity: Ask questions to find classmates who have things in common with you
Different hobbies ▪ Match four conversations about hobbies with photos, and fill in a chart *Favorite Web sites* ▪ Listen for details as two people talk about a Web site	▪ A Web page for hobby groups	▪ Write an e-mail message to one of the hobby groups on the Web page ▪ Link ideas with *and, also, especially, or, but,* and *because*	*I really like to sing!* ▪ Link new words together in word "chains"	*The game of likes and dislikes* ▪ Group work: Each person fills out a chart. Then groups compare answers and score points for finding things in common.
Unhealthy habits ▪ Predict what four people will say about their bad habits, and then listen for the exact words *Time to chill out* ▪ Match four conversations about relaxing with photos, and listen for details	▪ A leaflet about stress from the Department of Health	▪ Write a question asking advice about a health problem, and write replies to your classmates' questions ▪ Commas after *if* and *when* clauses	*Under the weather* ▪ Write down words you can use with a new word or expression	*Are you taking care of your health?* ▪ Pair work: Answer a health questionnaire with your partner, and figure out your partner's score

Touchstone checkpoint Units 1–3   pages 31–32

Celebrations around the world ▪ Listen to people talk about two festivals, and answer questions *Congratulations!* ▪ Listen for details in two conversations about invitations, and fill in the blanks	*Time to celebrate!* ▪ An article about traditions in different countries	▪ Write an invitation to a special event, and add a personal note ▪ Formal and informal ways to begin and end a note or letter	*Calendars* ▪ Write new vocabulary about special days and celebrations on a calendar	*A new celebration* ▪ Group work: Create a new special day or festival, and talk about it with other groups
I don't remember exactly . . . ▪ Listen for corrections people make as they talk about childhood memories *A long time ago* ▪ Listen for details as a man talks about his teenage years	*An interview with . . . Jennifer Wilkin* ▪ An interview with a woman who talks about her teenage years	▪ Write interview questions to ask a classmate about when he or she was younger, and reply to a classmate's questions ▪ Link ideas with *except (for)* and *apart from*	*I hated math!* ▪ Group new vocabulary in different ways	*In the past* ▪ Class activity: Ask your classmates questions about their childhood, and take notes
Finding your way around ▪ Match four sets of directions with the destinations by following the map *Tourist information* ▪ Listen to conversations at a tourist-information desk, and predict what each person says next to check the information	*A walking tour of San Francisco's Chinatown* ▪ Pages from a walking-tour guide	▪ Write a guide for a walking tour of your city or town ▪ Expressions for giving directions	*Which way?* ▪ Draw and label a map to remember directions	*Summer fun* ▪ Pair work: Ask and answer questions about two different resorts, and choose one for a vacation

Touchstone checkpoint Units 4–6   pages 63–64

	Functions / Topics	Grammar	Vocabulary	Conversation strategies	Pronunciation
Unit 7 **Going away** pages 65–74	• Talk about things you need to do before a trip • Give advice and make suggestions • Talk about travel and vacations	• Infinitives for reasons • *It's* + adjective + *to . . .* • Ways to give advice and make suggestions	• Things to do before a trip • Things to take on different kinds of trips	• Respond to suggestions • Use *I guess* when you're not sure	• Reduction of *to*
Unit 8 **At home** pages 75–84	• Talk about where you keep things at home • Talk about home furnishings • Identify objects • Talk about home habits and evening routines	• *Whose . . . ?* and possessive pronouns • Order of adjectives • Pronouns *one* and *ones* • Location expressions after pronouns and nouns	• Places where you keep things in your home • Home furnishings for different rooms • Things you keep in your room	• Ask politely for permission to do things with *Do you mind . . . ?* • Ask someone politely to do something with *Would you mind . . . ?* • Agree to requests	• Reduction of grammatical words
Unit 9 **Things happen** pages 85–94	• Tell anecdotes about things that went wrong • Talk about accidents • Respond to anecdotes	• Past continuous statements • Past continuous questions • Reflexive pronouns	• Parts of the body • Injuries	• React to and comment on a story • Respond with *I bet . . .*	• Fall-rise intonation

Touchstone **checkpoint Units 7–9**   **pages 95–96**

	Functions / Topics	Grammar	Vocabulary	Conversation strategies	Pronunciation
Unit 10 **Communication** pages 97–106	• Talk about different ways of communicating • Compare ways of keeping in touch • Manage phone conversations	• Comparative adjectives • *More*, *less*, and *fewer*	• Ways of communicating • Adjectives • Phone expressions	• Interrupt and restart phone conversations • Use *just* to soften things you say	• Linking
Unit 11 **Appearances** pages 107–116	• Describe people's appearances • Identify people	• Questions and answers to describe people • *have got* • Phrases with verb + *-ing* and prepositions to identify people	• Adjectives and expressions to describe people's appearances	• Show you're trying to remember a word or name • Use *You mean . . .* or *Do you mean . . . ?* to help someone remember something	• Checking information
Unit 12 **Looking ahead** pages 117–126	• Talk about the future • Talk about plans and organizing events • Discuss different jobs	• Future with *will*, *may*, and *might* • Present continuous and *going to* for the future • Clauses with *if, when, after,* and *before* and the simple present to refer to the future	• Work, study, and life plans • Occupations	• Make offers and promises with *I'll* and *I won't* • Agree to something with *All right* and *OK*	• Reduction of *will*

Touchstone **checkpoint Units 10–12**   **pages 127–128**

Listening	Reading	Writing	Vocabulary notebook	Free talk
It's good to travel. ▪ Predict what people are going to say about traveling, and then listen for the exact words *Recommendations* ▪ Match advice about staying at three unusual hotels with pictures; then listen to a radio show to check your answers	*Somewhere different . . .* ▪ An article about three unusual hotels	▪ Write a postcard about staying at one of the hotels in the lesson ▪ Format and expressions for writing a postcard	*Travel items* ▪ When you write down a new noun, write notes about it	*Travel smart!* ▪ Role play: Choose a role and give your partner travel advice according to the pictures
Could I ask a favor? ▪ Listen to four conversations between roommates, complete their requests, and then check if each person agrees *Evening routines* ▪ Listen to someone describe his evening routine, and number pictures in order	*At home – How typical are you?* ▪ An article about home habits of typical Americans	▪ Write a short article about the evening routines of the people in your group ▪ Order events using sequencing words	*The ABCs of home* ▪ Write down a word for something in your home for each letter of the alphabet	*All about home* ▪ Group work: Discuss questions about your homes, and find out what you have in common
Funny stories ▪ Listen to four anecdotes, and match each with a response *Happy endings* ▪ Listen to two anecdotes, and answer questions about the details	*Around town* by Nelson Hunter ▪ A newspaper column featuring letters from readers	▪ Write a letter to the newspaper column telling about something good that happened to you recently ▪ Link ideas with *when* and *while*	*From head to toe* ▪ Draw and label pictures to remember new vocabulary	*What was happening?* ▪ Pair work: Look at a picture for one minute, and see how much detail you can remember about what was happening

Touchstone **checkpoint Units 7–9**   **pages 95–96**

Listening	Reading	Writing	Vocabulary notebook	Free talk
Sorry about that! ▪ Listen to three phone conversations to infer the reason for each call and for each interruption *Text messaging* ▪ Listen to a teenager talk about text messaging, and check the opinions she agrees with	*C U L8R* ▪ An article about text messaging	▪ Write a short article on the advantages and disadvantages of a means of communication ▪ Structure of an article comparing advantages and disadvantages	*Phone talk* ▪ Learn new expressions by making note of the situations when you can use them	*Which is better?* ▪ Pair work: Compare pairs of items, and discuss which is better and why
Celebrities ▪ Listen to descriptions of celebrities, and match them with their photos *Next year's fashions* ▪ Listen to a fashion editor answer questions about next year's styles, and fill in a chart	*Hairstyles through the decades . . .* ▪ An article about hairstyles from the '50s through the '90s	▪ Write a fashion article describing the current "look" ▪ Expressions to describe new trends	*What do they look like?* ▪ Use new vocabulary in true sentences about yourself or people you know	*What's different?* ▪ Pair work: Ask and answer questions to determine what's different about people in two pictures, and guess where they went
Promises, promises ▪ Listen to two people organizing a class reunion, and identify what each of them says they'll do *I can't wait!* ▪ Listen to two people discussing predictions, and identify which person says each is a good idea and why	*What will life be like in the future?* ▪ An article with predictions about the future	▪ Write an article about how one of the predictions will make our lives better or worse ▪ List ideas with *First, Second, Next,* and *Finally*	*Writers, actors, and artists* ▪ Write new vocabulary in groups by endings, meanings, or topics	*I might do that.* ▪ Class activity: Interview classmates to find out about their future plans

Touchstone **checkpoint Units 10–12**   **pages 127–128**

Useful language for . . .

Getting help

How do you say "_____" in English?

I'm sorry. What did you say?

How do you say this word?

What do we have to do?

I don't understand. What do you mean?

Do you mean _____ ?

Can you spell "_____" for me, please?

Working with a partner

Whose turn is it now?

It's my / your turn.

Who goes first, A or B?

A does. That's me / you.

This time we change roles.

Are we done?

OK. I'll start.

Yes, I think so. Let's try it again.

Let's compare answers.

OK. What do you have for number 1?

Do you have _____ for number 3?

No, I have _____ . Let's check again.

Do you understand this sentence?

Yeah. It means "_____ ."

Making friends

In Unit 1, you learn how to . . .
- use the simple present and present of *be* (review).
- give responses with *too* and *either*.
- talk about yourself, your family, and your favorite things.
- start a conversation with someone you don't know.
- use *actually* to give or "correct" information.

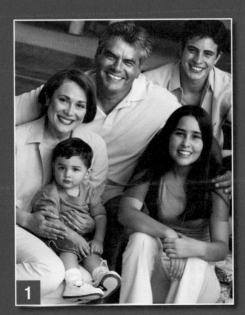

2

1

4

3

Before you begin . . .
Imagine you want to get to know someone.
What questions can you ask about each topic?

- home and family
- work
- studies
- free time

Getting to know you

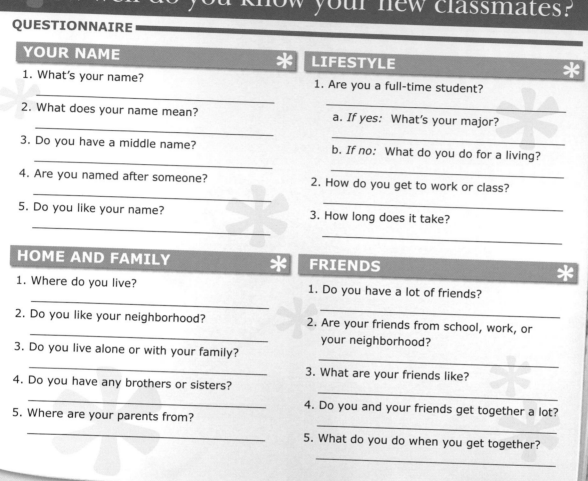

How well do you know your new classmates?

QUESTIONNAIRE

YOUR NAME *

1. What's your name?
_____

2. What does your name mean?
_____

3. Do you have a middle name?
_____

4. Are you named after someone?
_____

5. Do you like your name?
_____

LIFESTYLE *

1. Are you a full-time student?

   a. *If yes:* What's your major?
   _____

   b. *If no:* What do you do for a living?
   _____

2. How do you get to work or class?
_____

3. How long does it take?
_____

HOME AND FAMILY *

1. Where do you live?
_____

2. Do you like your neighborhood?
_____

3. Do you live alone or with your family?
_____

4. Do you have any brothers or sisters?
_____

5. Where are your parents from?
_____

FRIENDS *

1. Do you have a lot of friends?
_____

2. Are your friends from school, work, or your neighborhood?
_____

3. What are your friends like?
_____

4. Do you and your friends get together a lot?
_____

5. What do you do when you get together?
_____

1 Getting started

Pair work Use the questionnaire to interview each other. Write your partner's answers. Then tell the class one interesting thing about your partner.

"Marcella has seven brothers and sisters."

2 Speaking naturally *Stress and intonation*

Do you have a nickname?   Are you from a big family?   What do you do for fun?

Yes. People call me Jimmy.   Yes. I have four sisters.   I go to the movies.

A 🔊 Listen and repeat the questions and answers above. Notice the stress on the important content word. Notice how the voice rises, or rises and then falls, on the stressed word.

B *Pair work* Ask and answer the questions. Give your own answers.

3 Grammar *Simple present and present of **be** (review)*

Are you from a big family?
  Yes, I **am**. I'm one of six children.
  No, I'**m not**. There are only two of us.

Are you and your friends full-time students?
  Yes, we **are**. We're English majors.
  No, we'**re not**. We're part-time students.

What'**s** your name? **Is** it Leo?
  Yes, it **is**. My name'**s** Leo Green.
  No, it'**s not**. My name **isn't** Leo. It'**s** Joe.

Where **are** your parents from? **Are** they from Peru?
  Yes, they **are**. They'**re** from Lima.
  No, they'**re not**. My parents **aren't** from Peru.

Do you **have** any brothers and sisters?
  Yes, I **do**. I have a brother.
  No, I **don't**. I'm an only child.

Do you and your friends **get** together a lot?
  Yes, we **do**. We go out all the time.
  No, we **don't**. We don't have time.

What **does** your brother **do**? **Does** he **go** to college?
  Yes, he **does**. He **goes** to the same college as me.
  No, he **doesn't**. He **works** at a bank.

Where **do** your parents **live**? **Do** they **live** nearby?
  Yes, they **do**. They **live** near here.
  No, they **don't**. They **don't live** around here.

A Think of a possible question for each answer. Compare with a partner.

1. *A* ___What's your favorite color?___
   B Red.

2. *A* _____ ?
   B No, I'm not. I have one sister.

3. *A* _____ ?
   B No, I don't. I don't drive.

4. *A* _____ ?
   B He works in a store.

5. *A* _____ ?
   B We usually go out to dinner or see a movie.

6. *A* _____ ?
   B No, they don't. They don't have time.

7. *A* _____ ?
   B No, I hate mornings. I'm not a morning person.

8. *A* _____ ?
   B Well, I have a part-time job. I work Saturdays.

About you → **B** *Pair work* Ask and answer the questions. Give your own answers.

4 Listening and speaking *What's the question?*

A Listen to Tom's answers to these questions. Number the questions 1 to 6.

| ☐ *"Do you have any pets?"* | **1** *"What's your favorite name?"* | ☐ *"Who's your favorite actor?"* |
| ☐ *"What do you do on weeknights?"* | ☐ *"When do you spend time with your family?"* | ☐ *"Do you go out a lot on weekends?"* |

About you → **B** *Group work* Choose one of the questions, and tell the group your answer.
Then answer a follow-up question from each person in your group.

"My favorite name is Jennifer." ➡ *"How do you spell that?"*
"Why do you like that name?"
"Do you have a favorite boy's name?"

Lesson B Things in common

1 Building language

A Listen. What do these friends have in common? Practice the conversations.

①

A Dogs are so noisy, and they always wreck things. I'm just not an animal lover, I guess.
B Well, I'm not either. I'm allergic to dogs and cats.

②

A I don't watch much television.
B No, I don't either.
A I mean, I watch pro football.
B Yeah, I do too. But that's about it.

③

A I love shopping. I can shop for hours! Too bad I can't afford anything new.
B I know. I can't either. I'm broke.
A Yeah, I am too.

Figure it out

B Can you complete the answers? Use the conversations above to help you.

① A I'm not a football fan.
  B I'm _____ either.

② A I love shopping.
  B I _____ too.

③ A I can't have a pet.
  B I can't _____ .

2 Grammar *Responses with too and either*

I'm allergic to cats.	**I watch** pro football.	**I can** shop for hours!
I am too.	**I do too.**	**I can too.**
I'm not an animal lover.	**I don't** watch much television.	**I can't** afford anything new.
I'm not either.	**I don't either.**	**I can't either.**

People also respond with Me too and Me neither (or Me either).

A Respond to these statements using *too* or *either*. Then practice with a partner.

1. I watch a lot of TV.   *I do too.*
2. I'm allergic to some foods.
3. I can't afford a new car.
4. I'm not a sports fan.
5. I don't have a pet.
6. I can shop all day.

> **In conversation . . .**
>
> People actually say **Me either** more often than **Me neither**.
>
> ▇▇▇▇ **Me either.**
> ▇ **Me neither.**

About you

B *Pair work* Student A: Make the statements above true for you.
Student B: Give your own responses.

"I don't watch a lot of TV."   *"I don't either."* **or** *"Really? I watch TV all the time."*

3 Building vocabulary

A Brainstorm! How many words can you think of for each topic? Make a class list.

TV shows   **clothes**   **food**   **weekend activities**

Word sort → **B** Complete the chart with your favorites from the class list. Compare with a partner. Then tell the class what you and your partner have in common.

My favorite . . .

weekend activities	TV shows	food	clothes
sleep late			

A **I sleep late on the weekends.**
B **I do too.**   ➡   **"We both sleep late on the weekends."**

About you → **C** Complete the sentences with your likes and dislikes. Then tell your classmates your sentences. Find someone who feels the same way.

Who has the same tastes as you?

My likes and dislikes	Classmate who feels the same way
1. I can't stand _____ . (type of TV show)	_____
2. I often _____ . (weekend activity)	_____
3. I love to wear _____ . (item of clothing)	_____
4. I don't like _____ too much. (color)	_____
5. I'm not a _____ fan. (sport)	_____
6. I hate _____ . (type of food)	_____

"I can't stand soap operas. How about you?"   *"I can't either."*

4 Vocabulary notebook *Webs of words*

See page 10 for a new way to log and learn vocabulary.

Do you come here a lot?

1 Conversation strategy *Starting a conversation*

A Which topics can you talk about when you meet someone for the first time?
Check (✓) the boxes below.

☐ your salary   ☐ your family   ☐ the weather   ☐ someone's appearance
☐ your health   ☐ where you live   ☐ your problems   ☐ things you see around you

Now listen. What are Eve and Chris talking about?

Eve	**Ooh, it's cold tonight.**
Chris	**Yeah, it is. But actually, I kind of like cold weather.**
Eve	**You do? Really? . . . Boy, there are a lot of people out here tonight.**
Chris	**Yeah, it gets pretty crowded on weekends.**
Eve	**Do you come here a lot?**
Chris	**Yeah, I do, actually.**
Eve	**So are you a big hip-hop fan?**
Chris	**Yeah, I am. Are you?**
Eve	**Actually, no, but my brother's in the band tonight.**
Chris	**Oh, really? Cool. . . . By the way, my name's Chris.**
Eve	**Nice to meet you. I'm Eve.**

Notice how Eve starts a conversation with a stranger. She talks about the things around them, like the weather and the club, and asks general questions. Find examples in the conversation.

> *"Ooh, it's cold tonight."*
> *"Do you come here a lot?"*

B *Pair work* Think of a way to start a conversation for each situation. Compare with a partner. Then role-play the situations. Continue each conversation as long as you can.

1. You meet someone new at a party. The food is really good.   *"This food is delicious!"*
2. It's a very hot day. You're just arriving at a new class.
3. You're in a long line at a movie theater. It's a cold day.
4. You're working out at a new gym. The music is very loud.
5. You're in a new English class. You meet someone during the break.
6. You're at the bus stop on a beautiful day. Someone arrives and smiles at you.

SELF-STUDY
AUDIO CD
CD-ROM

2 *Strategy plus* Actually

You can use ***actually*** to give new or surprising information.

Do you come here a lot?

Yeah, I do, actually.

You can also use ***actually*** to "correct" things people say or think.

A So, you're American?
B Well, *actually*, I'm from Canada.

▶ *In conversation . . .*

Actually is one of the top 200 words.

A Match each conversation starter with a response. Then practice with a partner.

1. I like your jacket. __d__
2. Do you come here by bus? _____
3. Is that your newspaper? _____
4. Do you like this class? _____
5. Do you live around here? _____
6. Boy, it's warm in here. _____

a. Actually, I feel a bit cold.
b. Yeah. I actually look forward to it.
c. No, I walk, actually. It takes an hour.
d. Thanks. It's from Peru, actually.
e. Um . . . actually, no, it's not. Go ahead and take it.
f. Yes, right around the corner, actually.

About you

B *Pair work* Start conversations using the ideas above. Use *actually* in your responses if you need to.

"I like your watch."   *"Thanks. It was my grandfather's, actually."*

3 *Listening* Sally's party

A Listen to six people talk at Sally's party. Which conversation starters are the people responding to? Number the sentences.

[ ] *"Gosh, the music really is loud, huh?"*

[ ] *"Mmm. The food looks good."*

[ ] *"This is a great party."*

[ ] *"Are you a friend of Sally's?"*

[1] *"Is it me, or is it really hot in here?"*

[ ] *"I don't really know anyone here. Do you?"*

B Now listen to the complete conversations. Check your answers. What do you find out about Sally?

4 *Free talk* Me too!

See *Free talk 1* at the back of the book for more speaking practice.

1 Reading

A Which of these are good suggestions for social conversations?
Check (✔) the boxes. Then tell the class.

☐ Don't look at the other person.
☐ Keep quiet when the other person is talking.
☐ Ask questions that start with *what, where, how,* or *when.*

☐ Have some good topics to discuss.
☐ Talk about yourself a lot.

B Read the magazine article. What does it say about the suggestions above?
Do you agree with all of the ideas in the article?

How to improve your conversation skills

Do you like to meet new people? Do you like to talk, or are you shy? Whatever your answers, this guide can help you improve your conversation skills.

1 **Have some topics ready to start a conversation.** Say something about the weather or the place you're in. Talk about the weekend – we all have something to say about weekends!

2 **Make the conversation interesting.** Know about events in the news. Read restaurant and movie reviews. Find out about the current music scene or what's new in fashion or sports.

3 **Be a good listener.** Keep eye contact and say, "Yes," "Hmm," "Uh-huh," "Right," and "I know." And say, "Really? That's interesting." It encourages people to talk.

4 **Don't be boring.** Don't just say, "Yes" or "No" when you answer a question. Give some interesting information, too.

5 **Don't talk all the time.** Ask, "How about you?" and show you are interested in the other person, too. People love to talk about themselves!

6 **Ask information questions.** Ask questions like "What do you do in your free time?" or "What kind of food do you like?" Use follow-up questions to keep the conversation going. But don't ask too many questions – it's not an interrogation!

7 **Be positive.** Negative comments can sound rude. And if you don't want to answer a personal question, simply say, "Oh, I'm not sure I can answer that," or "I'd rather not say."

8 **Smile!** Everyone loves a smile. Just be relaxed, smile, and be yourself.

C Look at the article again. Find these things. Then compare with a partner.

1. an interesting topic of conversation
2. an example of an information question
3. a suggestion you would like to try
4. a question to show you're interested in the other person
5. something you can say to show you're listening
6. something to say if someone asks you a difficult question

2 Speaking and writing *How to improve your . . .*

A *Pair work* Brainstorm ideas for each topic, and make notes.

How to improve your social life	How to improve your English	How to improve your study skills
Go out. Be friendly.		
Take up a sport or hobby.		

B Choose one of the topics above, and use your ideas to write a short magazine article like the example below.

○○○   Document 1   ⊖

How to Improve Your Social Life

Do you feel lonely? Do you want to make new friends? Here are some ideas to help you.

1. Be friendly. Talk to people at school and work. Smile and say, "Hi. How are you?" to new people.

2. Go out a lot. Go to coffee shops, bookstores, clubs, and sports events. Try to start conversations with people around you.

> **Help note**

Punctuation

- Use a CAPITAL letter to start a sentence.
- Use a comma (**,**) before quotation marks (**" "**) and in lists.
- Use a period (**.**) at the end of a statement and a question mark (**?**) at the end of a question.

3 Talk about it *Friendly conversation*

Group work Discuss the questions. Find out about your classmates' conversation styles.

► Do you ever start conversations with strangers?
► Do you think it's odd when a stranger talks to you?
► Are you a talkative person?
► Do you think you talk too much?
► Are you a good listener?
► Are you usually the "talker" or the "listener" in a conversation?
► What do you like to talk about?
► What topics do you try to avoid?

Vocabulary notebook

Learning tip *Word webs*

> You can use word webs to organize your new vocabulary.

1 Complete the word webs for *clothes* and *food* using words from the box.

✓jacket   bread   skirt   sweatshirt   pineapple   jeans   rice   yogurt

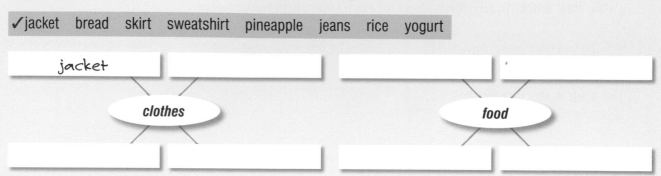

jacket

clothes

food

2 Now make word webs about *colors* and *TV shows*. Write a sentence about each word.

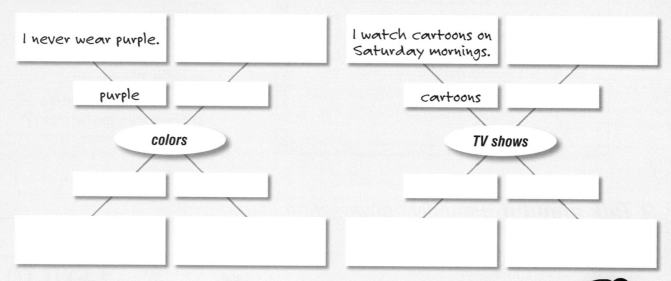

I never wear purple.

purple

colors

I watch cartoons on Saturday mornings.

cartoons

TV shows

On your own

> Choose a letter of the alphabet.
> Think of words that begin with that letter.
> Think of: a color
>   a food
>   an activity
>   an item of clothing
> Then make a sentence using the four words.

I play tennis and eat pineapple in pink pants.

Interests

In Unit 2, you learn how to . . .

- use different verb forms.
- use object pronouns, and the pronouns *everybody* and *nobody*.
- talk about your hobbies, interests, and taste in music.
- say *no* in a friendly way.
- use *really* and *not really* to make statements stronger or softer.

Before you begin . . .

Look at the magazine covers. Which magazines would you like to buy? Why?

Leisure time

College News

Meet our new reporter for the *College News*. . . .

The *College News* interviewed Eric Kane, our new reporter. Eric is a full-time student majoring in journalism. We asked him about his hobbies.

❶ *College News:* What are your hobbies?

Eric Kane: Well, I enjoy writing. I like to do a bit of creative writing every day – in the evenings mostly. Someday I want to write a novel, but for now it's just a hobby.

❸ *CN:*

EK: Yeah, I play the saxophone, and I can play the piano a little, but not very well. I'd like to play in a jazz band or something. And I like to sing, but I really can't sing at all.

❷ *CN:*

EK: Let's see, what else? Well, I design cards. I'm good at drawing, and I'm really into computer graphics, so I sit and learn new programs, and I play around with them.

❹ *CN:*

EK: Not really. I prefer to watch sports on TV. I like to play pool. Is that a sport? I guess I jog occasionally. But I hate going to the gym and working out.

❺ *CN:*

EK: Yeah. I love to do new stuff all the time – learn new skills, you know. I'm really excited about writing for the *College News*.

1 Getting started

A Listen to Eric's answers in the interview above. What are the questions? Number the questions, and add them to the interview.

- [ ] Are you good at sports?
- [ ] Are you interested in learning new things?
- [ ] Can you play a musical instrument?
- [ ] What else do you enjoy doing in your free time?
- [1] What are your hobbies?

B Listen to the complete interview. What does Eric like to do? What does he hate doing?

Figure it out → **C** Can you complete these sentences with verbs? Which sentences are true for you? Tell a partner.

1. I can _____ the piano.
2. I like _____ sports on TV.
3. I enjoy _____ to music.
4. I'm not good at _____ new computer programs.

2 Grammar Verb forms

Verb	to + verb	Verb + -ing	Preposition + verb + -ing
I can **play** the piano.	I love **to swim**.	I love **swimming**.	I'm good **at drawing** people.
I can't **play** very well.	I like **to play** pool.	I like **playing** pool.	I'm not interested **in skiing**.
I can't **sing** at all.	I hate **to work out**.	I hate **working out**.	
	I prefer **to watch** TV.	I prefer **watching** TV.	
	I'd like **to play** jazz.	I enjoy **reading**.	

A Complete the questions and add two more.

1. Can you ___whistle___ (whistle)?
2. Do you enjoy _____ (cook)?
3. Are you good at _____ (skate)?
4. Do you like _____ (play) board games?
5. Can you _____ (swim)?
6. Are you interested in _____ (join) a meditation class?
7. Do you prefer _____ (exercise) alone or with friends?
8. Would you like _____ (learn) a martial art?
9. _____ ?
10. _____ ?

▶ **In conversation . . .**

I like / love / hate to + verb
is more common than
I like / love / hate + verb + -ing.

I like to . . .
I like . . .ing

I love to . . .
I love . . .ing

I hate to . . .
I hate . . .ing

B **Pair work** Ask and answer the questions. Give your own answers.

A Can you whistle?
B Not very well. What about you? Can you whistle?

3 Survey

A **Class activity** Ask your classmates about their interests and hobbies. Make notes.

What are your interests?

Find someone who . . .	Name	Notes
is a good dancer.	Marta	likes to dance the tango
likes to read or write poetry.		
enjoys driving.		
hates doing exercise.		
can ride a horse.		
is good at learning languages.		
would like to learn French.		
takes guitar lessons.		

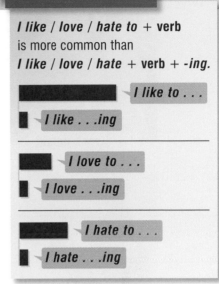

"Marta, are you a good dancer?"   *"Yes, I am. I like to dance the tango."*

B Tell the class about someone on your list.

"Marta is a good dancer. She likes to dance the tango."

1 Building vocabulary

A 💿 Listen. Number the types of music you hear. What other kinds of music do you know?

☐ rock music

1 hip-hop and rap

☐ pop music

☐ classical music

☐ country music

☐ folk music

☐ jazz

☐ Latin music

Word sort → **B** Complete the chart with the words above. Add ideas. Then compare with a partner.

I love . . .	I like . . .	I don't care for . . .	I can't stand . . .
rock music			

"I love rock music."   *"Yeah, I do too. And I love pop."*

2 Speaking naturally *Saying lists*

Jim What kinds of music do you like?

Sam I like classical, and hip-hop, and jazz.   *Sylvia I like pop, and rock, and folk, . . .*

A 💿 Listen and repeat the sentences above. Notice that Sam's list is complete, but Sylvia's list is not.

About you → **B** **Class activity** Ask your classmates *What kinds of music do you like?* Take notes. What are the three most popular answers?

3 Building language

A Listen. What does Carla think of the band? Practice the conversation.

Alex Listen. What do you think of this song?

Carla It's good – I like it. Who is it?

Alex A new band . . . some local guys. Do you like them?

Carla They're local? Really? They're pretty good. Who's the lead singer? I like her. She sounds like Mariah Carey.

Alex Yeah, everybody says that. It's my friend Lori.

Carla Who's the guy singing with her? I'm not sure about him.

Alex Uh . . . actually, that's me. I'm in the band, too.

> **Figure it out**

B Complete the conversations. Then ask a partner your questions. Give your own answers.

1 *A* What do you think of _____ (male singer)?

B I like _____ .

2 *A* Do you know _____ (female singer)?

B No, I don't know _____ .

4 Grammar *Object pronouns; everybody, nobody*

I'm a singer. That's **me** on the CD.	It's a nice song. I like **it**.	Everybody ⌉
You're a musician? I'd like to hear **you**.	**We** play in a band. Come listen to **us**.	Everyone ⎸ likes pop.
She's pretty good. I like **her**.	**They**'re local guys. Do you like **them**?	Nobody ⎹
He's not a good singer. I don't like **him**.		No one ⌋

A Complete the questions with object pronouns. Complete the answers with *everybody* or *nobody*. Then practice with a partner.

1. *A* I listen to hip-hop a lot. Do you listen to ___it___ , too?

   B Yes. ___Everybody___ in my school listens to hip-hop.

2. *A* Ricky Martin – he was on TV last night. Do you know _____ ?

   B Of course I do. _____ knows Ricky Martin.

3. *A* I don't really like classical music. Do you ever listen to _____ ?

   B Yes, but with earphones – _____ in my family likes it.

4. *A* I like Alicia Keys. She's a good singer. What do you think of _____ ?

   B Oh, almost _____ is a fan of Alicia Keys.

5. *A* My favorite band is Coldplay. I think they're great. Do you like _____ ?

   B Yeah. They're the best. _____ plays rock like they do.

> **In conversation . . .**
>
> **Everybody** and **nobody** are more common than **everyone** and **no one**.
>
> | | |
> |---|---|
> | ████████ | everybody |
> | █████ | everyone |
> | | |
> | ██ | nobody |
> | ██ | no one |

> **About you**

B *Pair work* Practice again with your own ideas.

"I listen to pop music a lot. Do you listen to it, too?"   *"Yes, I do. I think everybody likes pop music."*

5 Vocabulary notebook *I really like to sing!*

See page 20 for a new way to log and learn vocabulary.

Lesson C I really like making things.

1 Conversation strategy *Saying no in a friendly way*

A What can you add to this answer to make it sound friendly?

    A Do you have any hobbies?
    B No. _____ .

    Now listen. What hobbies do Sarah and Matt have?

Matt	**What are you knitting, Sarah?**
Sarah	**A sweater. It's for my brother.**
Matt	**Nice. Do you make a lot of things?**
Sarah	**Yeah. I really enjoy knitting. I guess it's my main hobby. Do you have any hobbies?**
Matt	**Um, no. I don't really have much time for hobbies. But I like to take photos. Do you do any photography?**
Sarah	**No, not really, um . . . I'm not really into photography. I prefer knitting, sewing, . . . I really like making things. But I'd love to see your pictures sometime.**
Matt	**Oh, well, I have some on my computer. Stop by my desk after lunch, and I can show them to you.**

Notice how Sarah and Matt say more than just no when they answer questions. They want to be friendly or polite, so they say more. Find examples in the conversation.

"Um, no. I don't really have much time for hobbies. But I like to . . ."

B Match the questions and answers. Then practice with a partner.

1. Do you have a lot of hobbies? _e_
2. Do you like making things? ____
3. Are you interested in cooking? ____
4. Are you into photography? ____
5. Can you knit or crochet? ____
6. Do you collect anything? ____
7. Are you good at fixing cars? ____

a. Um, no. I'm not really good with my hands.
b. Not really. I'm not very mechanical.
c. No, I don't. A friend of mine collects coins, though.
d. Well, no. I don't even have a camera.
e. No, not really. I don't have a lot of free time.
f. Not really, but I like to bake cakes and things.
g. No, but my sister can. She makes her own sweaters.

About you → **C** *Pair work* Ask and answer the questions. Give your own answers.

"Do you have a lot of hobbies?" *"Not really, but I enjoy shopping."*

SELF-STUDY
AUDIO CD
CD-ROM

2 Strategy plus *Really*

You can use *really* to make statements stronger and to make negative statements softer.

I really enjoy knitting.

I don't really have much time for hobbies.

Not really can also be a polite way to answer no.

> **In conversation . . .**
>
> The top verbs used with *really* are: *enjoy, like, know, think.*

About you ➔ **Pair work** Ask and answer the questions. Give your own answers using *really* or *not really.*

1. Are you interested in sports?
2. Are you into computers?
3. Do you enjoy doing jigsaw puzzles?
4. Are you good at doing crossword puzzles?
5. Can you do anything artistic, like draw or paint?
6. Would you like to learn a new skill, like carpentry?

A **Are you interested in sports?**
B **Well, I really like soccer.** **or** **Not really. I don't really play any sports.**

3 Listening *Different hobbies*

A Do you know anyone with these interests? Would you like to do any of these things? Tell the class.

collecting teddy bears

gardening

making jewelry

playing golf

B 💿 Listen to Jeff, Eva, Kim, and Phil. What are their hobbies? Write their names under the pictures.

C 💿 Listen again and complete the chart. You can check (✓) more than one name for each question. Then compare with a partner.

	Jeff	Eva	Kim	Phil
1. Who makes money on his / her hobby?	☐	☐	☐	☐
2. Who spends a lot of money on it?	☐	☐	☐	☐
3. Who isn't very good at his / her hobby?	☐	☐	☐	☐
4. Who isn't very enthusiastic about it?	☐	☐	☐	☐

Hobby groups

1 Reading

A Look at the hobby groups on this Web page. Which ones are you interested in?
Tell the class.

Hobby Group Message Board

Hobby Group Message Board

Find a group. [ ] (Search)

(Cars) (Collecting) (Cooking) (Crafts) (Fashion) (Music) (Outdoors) (Pets)

B Now read these messages. Can you match each message to one of the hobby groups above?

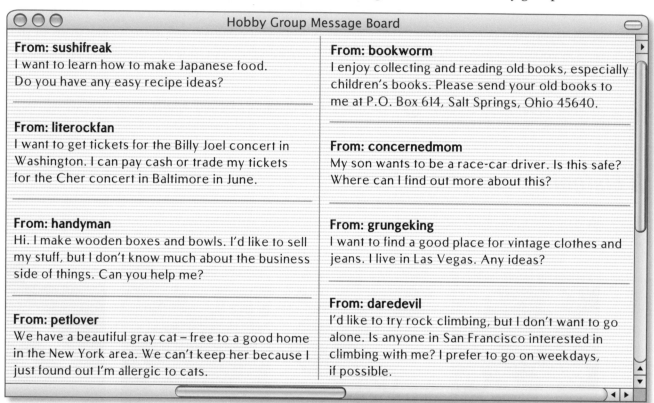

Hobby Group Message Board

From: sushifreak
I want to learn how to make Japanese food.
Do you have any easy recipe ideas?

From: literockfan
I want to get tickets for the Billy Joel concert in
Washington. I can pay cash or trade my tickets
for the Cher concert in Baltimore in June.

From: handyman
Hi. I make wooden boxes and bowls. I'd like to sell
my stuff, but I don't know much about the business
side of things. Can you help me?

From: petlover
We have a beautiful gray cat – free to a good home
in the New York area. We can't keep her because I
just found out I'm allergic to cats.

From: bookworm
I enjoy collecting and reading old books, especially
children's books. Please send your old books to
me at P.O. Box 614, Salt Springs, Ohio 45640.

From: concernedmom
My son wants to be a race-car driver. Is this safe?
Where can I find out more about this?

From: grungeking
I want to find a good place for vintage clothes and
jeans. I live in Las Vegas. Any ideas?

From: daredevil
I'd like to try rock climbing, but I don't want to go
alone. Is anyone in San Francisco interested in
climbing with me? I prefer to go on weekdays,
if possible.

C Look at the first line of these replies to the messages. Who are they for? Write the screen names.

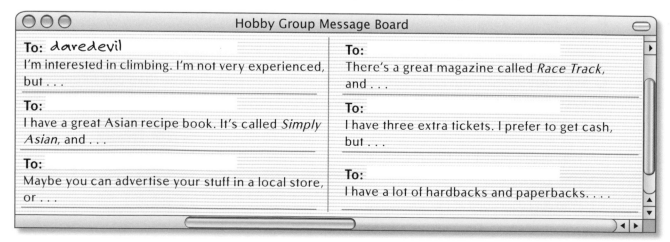

Hobby Group Message Board

To: daredevil
I'm interested in climbing. I'm not very experienced,
but . . .

To:
I have a great Asian recipe book. It's called *Simply
Asian*, and . . .

To:
Maybe you can advertise your stuff in a local store,
or . . .

To:
There's a great magazine called *Race Track*,
and . . .

To:
I have three extra tickets. I prefer to get cash,
but . . .

To:
I have a lot of hardbacks and paperbacks. . . .

2 Listening and speaking *Favorite Web sites*

A  Listen to Joe and Lisa talk about a Web site. What kind of Web site is it? Why does Joe like it?

B Listen again. Choose the correct information to complete the sentences.

1. **25,000 / 55,000** people visit the Web site each day.
2. Joe likes to read the **articles / messages** on the site.
3. Today's article is about hiking in **the U.S. / different countries**.
4. Lisa prefers to **sleep in a tent / stay home**.
5. Joe wants to enter the competition to win a **bike / tent**.

C *Group work* Ask and answer the questions.

- What's your favorite Web site?
- What's interesting about it?
- What other Web sites do you go to a lot?
- Do you ever use Web sites for shopping? banking? doing research?
- Do you have your own Web page or Web site?

3 Writing *Messages*

A Choose a hobby group from the Web page on page 18. Write a question to post on the message board.

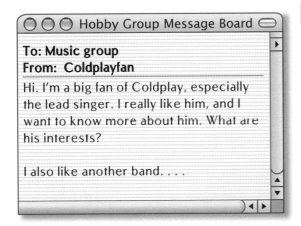

To: Music group
From: Coldplayfan
Hi. I'm a big fan of Coldplay, especially the lead singer. I really like him, and I want to know more about him. What are his interests?

I also like another band. . . .

> **Help note**
>
> **Linking ideas**
> - Add an idea:
>   *I listen to music, **and** I like movies.*
>   *I **also** like books, **especially** children's books.*
>   *I don't like jazz **or** rock music.*
> - Contrast two ideas:
>   *I like climbing, **but** my friends don't.*
> - Give a reason:
>   *We can't keep her **because** I'm allergic to cats.*

B Read your classmates' messages. Choose one and reply to it. Then "send" your reply. Do you receive any helpful replies?

4 Free talk *The game of likes and dislikes*

See *Free talk 2* at the back of the book for more speaking practice.

Vocabulary notebook

Learning tip *Word chains*

> Link new words together in word "chains."

The top 5 types of music
people talk about are:
1. rock   4. rap
2. classical   5. country
3. jazz

1 Complete the word chains using the words and expressions below.

| playing chess | bake cakes | listen to rock music |
| skiing | play the guitar | writing poetry |

I'm good at → [ ] and [ ] and [ ] .

I don't like to → [ ] or [ ] or [ ] .

2 Now complete the word chains with your own ideas.

I'm good at → [ ] and [ ] and [ ] .

I enjoy → [ ] and [ ] and [ ] .

I can't → [ ] or [ ] or [ ] .

I hate to → [ ] and [ ] and [ ] .

I'd like to → [ ] and [ ] and [ ] .

I'm not interested in → [ ] or [ ] or [ ] .

On your own

Think of different things you are
interested in. Can you link them
together? Use the last letter of each word
or expression to start the next word.

How many words did you use?

20

Health

In Unit 3, you learn how to . . .

- use the simple present and present continuous.
- use *if* and *when* in statements and questions.
- talk about health, remedies, sleep habits, and stress.
- encourage people to talk by making comments and asking follow-up questions.
- use expressions like *Wow!* and *You're kidding!* to show surprise.

Before you begin . . .

Which of these things do you do to stay healthy? What else can you do?

- Sleep at least seven hours a night.
- Get a checkup once a year.
- Take regular breaks to cope with stress.
- Eat plenty of fruit and vegetables.

Healthy living

Are you doing anything to stay healthy?

"Well, I generally don't eat a lot of junk food, and I don't eat red meat at all. And right now I'm doing karate. It's getting me in shape quick."

–Brian Jones

"Um . . . right now I'm trying to lose weight before my school reunion, so I'm drinking these diet drinks for dinner."

–Carmen Sanchez

"Well, I walk everywhere I go because I don't have a car, so I think I get enough exercise."

–Mei-ling Yu

"Um . . . to be honest, I'm not doing anything right now. I'm studying for exams this month, so I'm eating a lot of snacks, and I'm not getting any exercise at all."

–Michael Evans

"Not really. I kind of eat everything I want. I don't do anything to stay in shape. I'm just lucky, I guess."

–Lisa da Silva

"Yeah, we exercise six days a week. We go swimming every other day, and in between we go to the gym. And once in a while, we go hiking."

–The Parks

1 Getting started

A 🔘 Listen to these on-the-street interviews. Who do you think has a healthy lifestyle? Why?

Figure it out **B** Complete these sentences with a simple present or present continuous verb. Are the sentences true for you? Tell a partner.

1. I usually _____ to the gym twice a week.
2. This month, I _____ a lot of snacks.
3. I generally _____ healthy food.
4. I _____ karate right now.

2 Grammar *Simple present and present continuous*

Use the simple present to talk about "all the time" and routines.	Use the present continuous to talk about "now" and temporary events.

How **do** you **stay** in shape?
  I **walk** everywhere.
	What sports **are** you **playing** these days?
	  I**'m doing** karate. It**'s getting** me in shape.

Do you **get** regular exercise?
  Yes, I **do**. I **exercise** six days a week.
  No, we **don't**. We **don't exercise** at all.
	Is she **trying** to lose weight?
	  Yes, she **is**. She**'s drinking** diet drinks.
	  No, she**'s not**. She**'s not trying** to lose weight.

A Complete the conversations with the simple present or present continuous. Then practice with a partner.

> **In conversation . . .**
>
> The simple present is about 6 times more frequent than the present continuous, and even more frequent with *like*, *love*, *know*, *need*, and *want*.

1 *A* How _do_ you _cope_ (cope) with stress?

   B Well, I _____ (take) a course in aromatherapy right now, and I _____ (enjoy) it. But everybody in my family is pretty relaxed. We _____ (not get) stressed very often.

2 *A* What kind of exercise _____ you usually _____ (do)?

   B I _____ (like) swimming. My wife and I usually _____ (go) to the pool every day in the summer. Right now it's cold, so I _____ (not swim) at all. But my wife _____ (go) every day, even when it's cold.

3 *A* _____ you _____ (eat) a lot of fast food these days?

   B Well, I _____ (love) it, but right now I _____ (try) to eat a balanced diet. It's hard because my husband _____ (not like) fruit and vegetables.

About you → **B** *Pair work* Now ask and answer the questions. Give your own answers.

3 Listening and speaking *Unhealthy habits*

A These people are talking about their unhealthy habits. Try to guess what they're talking about. Then listen and write what they actually say.

1. Ian: "I'm trying to cut down on _____ and _____ ."
2. Kaylie: "I want to give up _____ , but I can't. It's very hard."
3. Martin: "I _____ everywhere. It's bad, I know. I never _____ ."
4. Silvia: "I _____ a lot. I _____ late almost every night."

B Listen again to the last thing each person says. Do you agree? Why or why not? Tell the class.

"I agree with Ian. I think it's good for you."   *"I don't agree with Ian because . . ."*

23

1 Building vocabulary

A 🎧 Listen and say the sentences. Do you have any of these problems right now?

I have **a fever.** I think I'm getting **the flu.**

I have **a bad cough.** I'm **coughing** a lot.

I have **a stomachache.** I often get stomachaches.

I have a **toothache.**

I hardly ever get **headaches,** but I have one now.

I have **a cold** and **a sore throat.** I get a lot of colds.

I feel **sick.** I often get sick when I eat shellfish.

I have **allergies** and I **sneeze** all the time.

Word sort

B Complete the chart with the words above. Add other ideas. Then compare with a partner.

I never . . .	I hardly ever . . .	I sometimes . . .	I often . . .
get colds			

"I never get colds. Thank goodness!"   *"You're lucky. I often get colds. But I never get the flu."*

2 Speaking naturally *Contrasts*

*A What's the matter? Do you have a **cold**?*
*B No, I have a **head**ache. I feel **te**rrible.*
*A That's too bad. I hope you feel **better.***
B Thanks.

A 🎧 Listen and repeat the conversation above. Notice how stress shows the contrast between *headache* and *cold*, and between *better* and *terrible*.

B *Pair work* Practice the conversation. Then practice again using different health problems.

3 Building language

A  Listen. What does Sonia want to make for Mark? Practice the conversation.

Mark   Hello?
Sonia   Hi, Mark. How are you feeling?
Mark   Awful. I still have this terrible cold.
Sonia   That's too bad. Are you taking anything for it?
Mark   Just some cold medicine.
Sonia   Hmm. I never take that stuff when I have a
cold. But if I get a really bad cold, I drink hot
vinegar with honey. I can make you some.
Mark   Oh, no thanks! I don't feel *that* bad!

B What do you do when you're sick? Complete the sentences.

1. I take medicine when _____ .
2. If I have a really bad cold, I _____ .

4 Grammar *Joining clauses with if and when*

What do you take **when** you have a cold?	What do you do **if** you get a really bad cold?
I don't take anything **when** I have a cold.	**If** I get a really bad cold, I drink hot vinegar with honey.
When I have a cold, I don't take anything.	I drink hot vinegar with honey **if** I get a really bad cold.

About you

A Join the phrases with *when* to make true sentences about yourself. Then compare with a partner.

1. have a fever / take medicine
2. get a stomachache / stay in bed
3. have a cough / go to the doctor
4. feel sick / lie down for a while
5. have a sore throat / drink hot tea with honey
6. have a headache / take aspirin

"When I have a fever, I usually take medicine."   *"Really? I never take medicine when I have a fever."*

B Find out what your classmates do in these situations. Use *if* in your questions and answers.

What do they do if they . . .
1. have a bad cold and have to go to class?
2. feel sore after exercising?
3. have a high fever?
4. have an upset stomach after they eat?
5. feel tired and run down?
6. have to cough or sneeze at a concert or movie?

A   **What do you do if you have a bad cold and have to go to class?**
B   **Well, if I have a bad cold, I usually take a lot of tissues to class.**
C   **Really? If I have a bad cold, I just stay home.**

5 Vocabulary notebook *Under the weather*

See page 30 for a new way to log and learn vocabulary.

How come you're tired?

1 Conversation strategy *Encouraging people to talk*

A Which are the best responses to keep the conversation going? Check (✓) the boxes.

A *I'm so tired.*

B
- [ ] Yeah, I know.
- [ ] Yeah. Me too.
- [ ] Really? How come?

- [ ] Oh! Why is that?
- [ ] Oh, I'm sorry.
- [ ] You look tired. Are you busy at work?

Now listen. Why is Adam tired?

Adam **I'm so tired.**

Yuki **Really? How come?**

Adam **Well, I'm working two jobs this semester, so I'm getting up at, like, 5:30 to study.**

Yuki **You're kidding! Two jobs? Wow.**

Adam **Yeah. Just for a couple of months. I'm working in a supermarket after class, and then I have my regular job at the restaurant till 11:00.**

Yuki **Oh, that's late. So, what time do you go to bed?**

Adam **About 1:00 . . . 1:30.**

Yuki **Gosh. So you're only getting about four hours' sleep? That's not much.**

Notice how Yuki encourages Adam to continue talking. She comments on what Adam says and asks follow-up questions. Find examples in the conversation.

"I'm so tired."

　　"Really? How come?"

B Match each sentence with an appropriate reply. Then practice with a partner.

1. I need a lot of sleep. __d__
2. I can't sleep if there's light in my room. _____
3. I usually go to bed early during the week. _____
4. If I can't fall asleep, I usually read. _____
5. I often take a nap after lunch. _____
6. I only sleep about five hours a night. _____

a. I can't either. Do your windows have blinds?
b. That's not much. Are you getting enough sleep?
c. At the office? How long do you sleep?
d. Really? How much sleep do you need?
e. That's good. Do you wake up early, too?
f. That's a good idea. What do you read?

About you → **C** *Pair work* Student A: Tell a partner about your sleep habits. Use the ideas above.
Student B: Respond with comments and questions. Then change roles.

A *I don't really need a lot of sleep.*
B *Really? Me neither. How much sleep do you need?*
A *About five hours a night.*

**SELF-STUDY
AUDIO CD
CD-ROM**

2 Strategy plus *Showing surprise*

Use expressions like these to show surprise in informal conversations:

Oh!	Gosh!
Really?	Oh, my gosh!
Wow!	You're kidding!
Oh, wow!	Are you serious?
No way!	No!

In formal conversations, use *Oh!* or *Really?*

I'm working two jobs.

You're kidding!

A Listen and write the expressions you hear. Then practice and continue the conversations with a partner.

In conversation . . .

Oh and *Really* are in the top 50 words. *Wow* and *Gosh* are in the top 500.

❶ *A* I love sleeping late on the weekends. I get up around 2:30 on Saturdays.

   B _____ ? _____ ! What time do you go to bed?

❷ *A* This magazine says too much sleep is bad for you.

   B _____ ? I sleep ten hours a night. Is that bad?

❸ *A* I have the same dream every night.

   B Every night? _____ ! What do you dream about?

B Listen to six people talk about their sleep habits. Respond with an expression from the box above.

1. _____   4. _____
2. _____   5. _____
3. _____   6. _____

3 Talk about it *Sweet dreams?*

Group work Discuss the questions about sleep habits. What do you have in common?

▶ Are you feeling tired today? If so, why?
▶ Do you sleep well, usually?
▶ What do you do if you can't sleep?
▶ Do you ever wake up during the night?
▶ What is your bedtime routine?

▶ Do you ever have vivid dreams or nightmares?
▶ Do you remember your dreams?
▶ Do you snore or talk in your sleep?
▶ Are you a sleepwalker?

4 Free talk *Are you taking care of your health?*

See ***Free talk 3*** for more speaking practice.

1 Reading

A Do you ever get stressed? How do you feel when that happens? Check (✓) the boxes and add ideas. Then tell the class.

I get stressed when . . .

☐ I'm studying for an exam.   ☐ I have a deadline.
☐ I'm late for an appointment.   ☐ _____ .
☐ I have no money.   ☐ _____ .

When I'm stressed, I . . .

☐ feel tired and irritable.
☐ get a headache.
☐ _____ .

B Read the leaflet. What do you learn about stress? Are any of your ideas mentioned?

COMMON QUESTIONS ABOUT STRESS

Am I stressed?

If you can't sleep well or can't concentrate, . . .

If you feel depressed or want to cry a lot, . . .

If you have a headache or an upset stomach, . . .

If you can't relax and you feel irritable, . . .

If you are extremely tired, . . .

. . . then it's possible you are stressed.

Is stress bad for me?

Occasional stress is common and can be good for you. However, if you feel stressed for a long time, it can be serious. Stress can make you sick. It can also affect your memory or concentration, so work or study is difficult.

What can I do?

Fortunately, there's a lot you can do. Try some of these relaxation techniques. If you still feel stressed, make an appointment to see your doctor.

RELAXATION TECHNIQUES

1 Breathe Take a breath, hold it for four seconds, and then breathe out very slowly. Feel your body relax.

2 Exercise Walk or exercise for just 30 minutes each day and feel better.

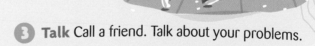

3 Talk Call a friend. Talk about your problems.

4 Meditate Close your eyes and focus on something calm. Feel relaxed.

5 Pamper yourself Take a hot bath, or have a massage.

6 Do something you enjoy Listen to music. Sing. Watch TV. Meet a friend.

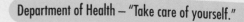
Department of Health – "Take care of yourself."

C Read the leaflet again. Answer the questions. Then compare answers with a partner.

1. How can you tell if you are stressed?
2. Why can stress be serious?
3. What can you do if you feel stressed?
4. Which relaxation ideas in the leaflet do you like?
5. Do you think the leaflet is helpful? Why or why not?

2 Listening *Time to chill out*

A What do you and your friends do to relax? Do you do any of these things? Tell a partner.

B Listen to four people talk about relaxing. Number the pictures.

C Listen again. What else do they do to relax? Write the activity under each picture.

3 Writing *Advice on health*

A Do you have a question about your health? Write a health problem on a piece of paper. Use the ideas below to help you.

> I'm feeling stressed about my exams. Help!

> I can't sleep at night. What can I do?

> I want to get in shape. What can I do?

> I get colds all the time. Any suggestions?

B *Group work* Pass your papers around the group. Write a reply to each person.

> I'm feeling stressed about my exams. Help! (Susana)
>
> If you're feeling stressed about your exams, imagine that you are taking the exam and that you are relaxed. (Mi Young)
>
> When you feel really stressed, go to the gym or swim. Exercise can help you! (Luis)

Help note

Commas after *if* and *when* clauses

- Use a comma here:
  If you're feeling stressed, try these ideas.
  When you feel stressed, go to the gym.

- Don't use a comma here:
  Go to the gym **when** you feel stressed.

Vocabulary notebook

Under the weather

Learning tip *Learning words together*

When you learn a new word or expression, write down other words you can use with it.

What's the matter?

The top 5 health problems people talk about are:

1. cold   4. flu
2. headache   5. fever
3. allergies

1 Complete these expressions. Use the words in the box.

a break	better	home	in bed	medicine	sick

feel		stay		take	

2 Which of these verbs can you use with the words and expressions in the chart? Complete the chart. You can use some verbs more than once.

be	do	feel	get	go (to)	have	see	stay	take

be feel get	sick		allergies		a vacation
	exercise		a headache		a cough
	a checkup		home		healthy
	stressed		in shape		a doctor

On your own

Go to a drugstore, and look at the medicine. What health problems are they for? Can you remember the names of the health problems in English?

People take this when they have a cough.

1 Can you complete this conversation?

Complete the conversation. Use the simple present or present continuous. Then practice with a partner.

Teri Hi. How __are__ you __doing__ (do)?

Ruth Not bad. Actually, I _____ (have) a cold again. But I'm OK.

Teri Oh, that's too bad. So, what _____ you _____ (do) today?

Ruth My classmate Sally's here. We _____ (plan) an end-of-term party.
Everybody _____ (want) some live music this year.
How about you? _____ you _____ (do) anything
special today? _____ you _____ (listen) to a CD?

Teri No, that _____ (be) my brother. He _____ (play)
his guitar. He _____ (practice) every morning.

Ruth Hey, _____ (be) he free on Saturday?
_____ he _____ (want) to play at our party?
We _____ (need) somebody like him.

Teri _____ you _____ (kid)? He's only ten!

2 How can you say no?

Add object pronouns to the sentences. Then ask and answer the questions. If your
answer is *no*, remember to say *no* in a friendly way.

1. I hate colds, and I get __them__ a lot. Do you get a lot of colds?
2. Some friends and I go to a jazz club every Monday. Do you want to join _____ next week?
3. I have to go to the hospital tomorrow. Can you come with _____ ?
4. My dad wants to paint the house next weekend. Can you help _____ ?
5. I love listening to Norah Jones. She's great! Do you like _____ , too?
6. I'm reading a book about the martial arts. Would you like to borrow _____ sometime?

"Do you get a lot of colds?"   *"Not really. I don't really get sick too often."*

3 How many words do you remember?

A Complete the chart. How many things can you think of for each column?

Types of music you really like	Types of TV shows you often watch	Hobbies you and your friends have	Clothes you don't like to wear	Health problems you sometimes get
rock				

B *Pair work* Take turns discussing the items in your chart. Encourage your partner to talk.

A Well, I really like rock music.
B Really? Who do you listen to? I mean, who are your favorite bands?

4 *What do you have in common?*

Complete the sentences with activities. Then compare with a partner. Continue your conversations.

1. I like _____ .
2. I don't enjoy _____ .
3. I'm not good at _____ .
4. I can't _____ .
5. I hate _____ .
6. I'm interested in _____ .

A *I like to play softball. How about you?*

B *Oh, I do too. I play on a team on weekends.*

A *Really? I just play with some friends after work. Actually, we have a game tonight. . . .*

5 *Surprise, surprise!*

Complete the conversation. Use the sentences in the box. Then practice with a partner.

What instruments do you play?	Are you serious?	✓How's school?
Not well, but I'd love to play in a band.	Yeah? I am too.	No way! What kind of music?
Me too. I have my first piano lesson today!	What do you want to do?	

Alice Hi, Carl. How are things?

Carl Great. <u>How's school?</u>

Alice Um, actually, I'm not at school this year.

Carl _____ So, what are you doing?

Alice Well, I'm looking for a job right now.

Carl Really? _____

Alice Well, I'd like to play music in clubs, but –

Carl _____

Alice Well, I play jazz.

Carl No! _____

Alice Saxophone and trumpet. But I really need to find someone to play with me.

Carl I play the piano. _____

Alice You play the piano? That's great. Maybe we can practice together sometime. I'm free this Friday.

Carl _____ What's your phone number?

Alice It's 555-9003. OK, so call me. Oh, look at the time. Sorry, I have to go.

Carl _____

6 *What can you say or do . . . ?*

A *Pair work* What can you say or do in these situations? Do you agree?

What can you say when . . .

- you meet your new neighbors for the first time?
- a new student joins the class and seems nervous?
- the person next to you on the subway looks sick?
- you meet someone interesting at a party?
- you have an umbrella at a bus stop on a rainy day, and the person next to you is getting very wet?

A *What can you say when you meet new neighbors for the first time?*

B *Let me think . . . "Hello." . . . "How are you?" . . . "Would you like some coffee?"*

B *Pair work* Choose a situation. Prepare a short conversation to act out for the class.

Self-check

How sure are you about these areas?
Circle the percentages.

grammar
20% 40% 60% 80% 100%

vocabulary
20% 40% 60% 80% 100%

conversation strategies
20% 40% 60% 80% 100%

. . . .

Study plan

What do you want to review?
Circle the lessons.

grammar
1A 1B 2A 2B 3A 3B

vocabulary
1A 1B 2A 2B 3A 3B

conversation strategies
1C 2C 3C

Celebrations

In Unit 4, you learn how to . . .

- use *going to* and the present continuous to talk about the future.
- use indirect object pronouns.
- talk about birthdays, celebrations, and favorite holidays.
- use "vague" expressions like *and everything*.
- give "vague" responses like *Maybe* and *It depends*.

Before you begin . . .

Which of these special events are the people celebrating?

- a graduation
- a wedding
- the birth of a baby
- an engagement
- a retirement
- a wedding anniversary

What other special days do people celebrate?

Months ▼

January	May	September
February	June	October
March	July	November
April	August	December

Days of the month ▼

1st	first	17th	seventeenth
2nd	second	18th	eighteenth
3rd	third	19th	nineteenth
4th	fourth	20th	twentieth
5th	fifth	21st	twenty-first
6th	sixth	22nd	twenty-second
7th	seventh	23rd	twenty-third
8th	eighth	24th	twenty-fourth
9th	ninth	25th	twenty-fifth
10th	tenth	26th	twenty-sixth
11th	eleventh	27th	twenty-seventh
12th	twelfth	28th	twenty-eighth
13th	thirteenth	29th	twenty-ninth
14th	fourteenth	30th	thirtieth
15th	fifteenth	31st	thirty-first
16th	sixteenth		

Alicia It's Mom's birthday on the first. Remember? She's going to be 50!

Dave Oh, that's right. What are you going to get her?

Alicia I'm going to buy her something special, like a necklace. Then it's Mom and Dad's anniversary on the tenth.

Dave Right. We usually give them something.

Alicia We? You mean, **I** do! Let's, um, send them some flowers.

Dave OK. Then it's my birthday on the twenty-third.

Alicia Yeah, I know. I'm going to get you the same thing you got me – nothing!

1 Getting started

A 💿 Listen and say the months and the days of the month. When is your birthday? Circle the month and the day. Tell the class.

"My birthday's in May." **or** *"My birthday's on May tenth."* **or** *"My birthday's on the tenth of May."*

B 💿 Listen. What gifts are Alicia and Dave going to buy? Practice the conversation.

Figure it out → **C** Can you complete the answer to the question? Then practice with a partner.

A What are you going to do for your next birthday?
B I think I'm _____ .

2 *Grammar* *Future with* **going to**; *indirect objects*

I'm	**going to** buy something special.	
You're	**going to** get a present.	
She's	**going to** be 50.	
We're	**going to** send some flowers.	
They're	**going to** have a party.	

What **are** you **going to** do for your birthday?
    I'm **not going to** do anything special.
Are you **going to** have a party?
    Yes, we **are**. We're **going to** invite all our friends.
    No, we're **not**. We're **not going to** do much.

Indirect objects
I'm going to buy **my mother** something special.
Alicia isn't going to give **Dave** anything.
Let's send **Mom and Dad** some flowers.

Indirect object pronouns:
me, you, him, her, us, them

I'm going to buy **her** something special.
Alicia isn't going to give **him** anything.
Let's send **them** some flowers.

About you → **A** Complete the questions using *going to*. Then write your own answers, using indirect object pronouns where necessary.

1. _____ you _____ do anything special for your next birthday?

2. _____ you _____ invite your friends over for a party?

3. _____ someone _____ bake you a birthday cake?

4. _____ your parents _____ buy you something nice?

5. How old _____ your parents _____ be on their next birthdays?

6. What _____ you _____ give your father for his birthday?
    How about your mother? And your best friend?

B *Pair work* Ask and answer the questions.

A **Are you going to do anything special for your next birthday?**
B **Yeah. My friends are going to buy me dinner at a Thai restaurant.**

3 *Speaking naturally* *going to*

What are you **going to** *do tonight?*   *Are you* **going to** *go to the movies?*   *I'm* **going to** *stay home.*

A Listen and repeat the sentences above. Notice the ways of saying *going to*.

About you → **B** Listen. Match the two parts of each question. Then ask a partner the questions.

1. Are you going to _e_
2. How many cards are you going to ____
3. Are you going to ____
4. Who are you going to ____
5. Are you going to ____

a. spend your next birthday with?
b. send anyone flowers this year?
c. send this year?
d. send anyone a card this month?
e. buy anyone a gift this month?

A **Are you going to buy anyone a gift this month?**
B **Yeah, my brother. His birthday is on the fifth. I think I'm going to buy him a watch.**

1 Building vocabulary

A What do people do on these special days? Find two expressions from the box for each event. What else do people do? Add ideas.

blow out candles on a cake	go out for a romantic dinner	shout "Happy New Year"
give someone chocolates	go to see fireworks	sing "Happy Birthday"
exchange rings	go trick-or-treating	wear a cap and gown
get a degree or diploma	have a reception	✓ wear a costume

1 Halloween

wear a costume
_____
_____
_____

2 Valentine's Day

_____
_____
_____

3 birthday

_____
_____
_____

4 graduation day

_____
_____
_____

5 New Year's Eve

_____
_____
_____

6 wedding day

_____
_____
_____

B *Pair work* Talk about special days or events you are going to celebrate this year. When are they? How are you going to celebrate them?

A *I'm going to have a Halloween party in October.*
B *Is everybody going to wear costumes?* *Are you going to go trick-or-treating, too?*

2 Building language

A  Listen to Marcella's phone message. What are her plans for New Year's Eve?

Voice mail Hi. This is Laurie. Please leave a message after the beep. Thanks for calling.

Marcella Hi, Laurie. This is Marcella. Listen, what are you doing tomorrow night? A group of us are going out for dinner and then to a big New Year's Eve party. Do you want to come? We're meeting at the restaurant at 8:30, and we're probably going to go to the party around 11:00. It's going to be a lot of fun. So call me back, OK? Oh, and by the way, they say it's going to snow tomorrow, so be careful. Bye.

Figure it out → **B** Find Marcella's plans. Find the weather prediction. What verb forms does she use?

3 Grammar *Present continuous for the future; going to*

You can use the present continuous or *going to* to talk about plans.
The present continuous is often used for plans with specific times or places.

What **are** you **doing** for New Year's Eve?
 We**'re going to** The Sea Grill for dinner.
 We**'re meeting** friends there at 8:30.

What **are** you **going to do** for New Year's Eve?
 We**'re going to go** somewhere for dinner.
 We**'re going to meet** some friends at a restaurant.

You can also use *going to* for predictions.

It's **going to** be fun. (NOT ~~It's being fun.~~) It's **going to** snow tomorrow. (NOT ~~It's snowing tomorrow.~~)

A Match each plan with a prediction. Then role-play with a partner. Ask follow-up questions.

1. My best friend's getting married in May. _c_
2. We're going trick-or-treating on Halloween. ____
3. My parents are going to get me something special for graduation. ____
4. My sister's graduating from law school soon. ____
5. I'm going to get my dad a tie for his birthday. ____

a. I think he's going to love it!
b. She's going to be a great lawyer.
c. It's going to be a fun wedding.
d. It's going to rain, but we don't care.
e. I think they're going to get me a laptop.

A *My best friend's getting married in May. It's going to be a fun wedding.*
B *Oh. Where are they having the reception?*

About you → **B** *Pair work* Find out about each other's plans for next weekend and the next holiday.

"What are you doing on Friday night?" *"I'm meeting a friend. We're going to go to a club."*

4 Vocabulary notebook *Calendars*

See page 42 for a new way to log and learn vocabulary.

Lesson C Festivals and things

1 Conversation strategy *"Vague" expressions*

A What do you think the underlined expression means? Check (✓) two ideas.

We have a lot of festivals <u>and things like that</u>.

☐ hobbies ☐ celebrations ☐ holidays

Now listen. What happens during the fiesta?

Ray	Are you going to the fiesta this weekend?
Tina	I don't know. It depends. What is it exactly?
Ray	Well, it's just, um . . . it's a festival. It's lots of parades and stuff like that. Everybody gets dressed up, you know. . . .
Tina	You mean in costumes?
Ray	Yeah. There are hundreds of cute little kids in purple and silver outfits with makeup and everything. . . .
Tina	Uh-huh. Uh, I'm not big on parades.
Ray	And there's good food. You can get all kinds of tacos and things. Do you want to go?
Tina	Hmm. Well, maybe.

Notice how Ray uses "vague" expressions like *and everything* and *and things (like that)*. He doesn't need to give Tina a complete list. Find examples in the conversation.

"You can get all kinds of tacos and things."

B What do the "vague" expressions mean in these conversations? Choose two ideas from the box for each one. Then practice with a partner.

In conversation . . .

People often say *and stuff* in very informal situations.

and stuff ■ ■ ■ ■ ■ ■ ■   *and things* ■ ■ ■

anniversaries	concerts	dancing	✓ holidays	sing "Happy Birthday"
candles	cultural events	folk songs	see old friends	spend time at home

❶ A Do you go to a restaurant to celebrate birthdays *and stuff*? holidays
  B Yeah, we know a nice place. They bring out cakes *and everything*.

❷ A Are you into traditional music *and stuff like that*?
  B Yeah, we have a lot of music festivals *and things like that* around here.

❸ A What are you doing for New Year's?
  B I'm going home. I really want to see my family *and everything*.

SELF-STUDY
AUDIO CD
CD-ROM

2 Strategy plus *"Vague" responses*

You can use responses like these if you're not sure about your answer:
I don't know.
I'm not sure.
Maybe.
It depends.

Are you going to the fiesta this weekend?

I don't know. It depends. What is it exactly?

> **In conversation . . .**
>
> *I don't know* and *I'm not sure* are more common responses than *Maybe* and *It depends.*

	I don't know.
	I'm not sure.
	Maybe.
	It depends.

Group work Choose a festival or holiday. Discuss the questions. Use "vague" responses if you need to.

- When is it?
- What does it celebrate?
- How do people celebrate?
- Do they eat any special foods?
- Do they wear costumes or put up decorations?
- How are you going to celebrate it next time?

A **What about Mardi Gras? Let's talk about that.**
B **OK. So, when is it?**
C **It depends. It's different every year.**

3 Listening *Celebrations around the world*

Look at the pictures of these two festivals. What's happening? Then listen and answer the questions.

	Santa Lucia Day	Bonfire Night
What country is it in?	It's in Sweden.	
When is it?		
What do people do?		

4 Free talk *A new celebration*

See *Free talk 4* for more speaking practice.

1 Reading

A Brainstorm! How many words can you think of related to these celebrations? Make a class list.

weddings   **birthdays**   **New Year's Eve**

weddings: bride, groom, flower girl

B Read the article. Which of your words can you find?

Time to celebrate!

New Year

Children in **Taiwan** love Chinese New Year because they know they are going to get *hong bao* from their relatives. *Hong bao* are red envelopes with money inside.

In **Ecuador**, people say good-bye to the old year by burning life-size dummies dressed in old clothes on big bonfires. Young people dress up as widows, witches, or skeletons and ask for money for fireworks for the New Year's celebrations.

Birthdays

In **Korea** on a baby's first birthday, parents put things like money, thread, and pencils in front of their baby. If the baby picks up the money, it means he or she is going to be rich. Choosing the thread means a long life for the baby, and choosing a pencil means he or she is going to be a good student.

Weddings

In **Colombia**, the bride and groom each light a candle. Then they light a third candle together and blow out the first two. This third candle means that they are now one and are going to share their lives together.

In the **United Kingdom**, **Australia**, and **North America**, brides wear "something old, something new, something borrowed, and something blue" for good luck.

In **Turkey**, the female friends of the bride write their names inside her shoes. After the wedding ceremony, the bride looks inside her shoes. If she can no longer read one of her friends' names, it means that friend is going to get married next.

C Read the article again. Can you find these things? Compare answers with a partner.

1. three traditions about money
2. three traditions about clothes
3. three traditions using fire
4. the words for two people who get married

  D *Group work* Discuss the questions about traditions.

■ What traditions do you have for weddings? What do brides wear?
■ Which birthdays are special? How do people celebrate them?
■ What traditions do you have for New Year's? What brings good luck?

2 *Listening and writing* Congratulations!

A Listen to the people open their invitations to these events. Complete the information.

❶

You're invited to
a housewarming party!

for ___Elaine Collins___
on _____
at _____ p.m.
at ___1452 E. Mulberry St.___

Hi Simon and Julie,
I'm finally ready to entertain! I'm having a barbecue. Sally is going to bring some _____. Simon, can you make some of your special _____?
Thanks!
See you then,   *Elaine*

❷

In celebration of their
_____ wedding anniversary,
Iris and Derek
invite you to dinner
on _____
at _____ p.m.
at The _____ Restaurant.
R.S.V.P.

Dear John and Jessie,
Hope you can make it to the dinner. There's going to be _____ and _____ afterwards.
We're looking forward to seeing you both.
Regards,
Iris and Derek

B Invite a friend to a special event. Write an invitation like the ones above, and add a personal note.

▶ *Help note*

Writing personal notes

	Less formal	*More formal*
Start like this:	*Dear* (name), *Hi* (name),	*Dear* (name),
End like this:	*Take care,* *See you,* *Love,*	*Best wishes,* *Best regards,* *All the best,*

C *Group work* Exchange invitations. Which invitation is the most popular in your group? Tell the class.

Vocabulary notebook

Calendars

Learning tip *Linking events with dates*

You can write down some of your new vocabulary on a calendar. It's a useful way to learn the names of special events and celebrations.

1 Complete the calendar with words from the box.

card	vacation	Eve	February	fireworks	November	graduation	anniversary
May	dinner	✓flowers	September	Halloween	retirement	Valentine's	gown

January
11th – *Mom's birthday. Buy her* __flowers__ *and a cake.*

_____ 14th – _____ *Day!*

March
23rd – *Suzanne's birthday. Go out for* _____ .

April
1st – *April Fools' Day*

_____ 4th – *My birthday!*

June
2nd – *End of exams*
21st – *School* _____ .
Rent a cap and _____ .

July
1st – *Summer* _____ *starts.*
22nd – *Dad's 65th birthday and* _____ *party*

August
16th – *Summer party and* _____ *at night*

_____ 10th – *Jack and Betty's wedding* _____ . *Send them a* _____ .

October
31st – _____

_____ 29th – *Family reunion for Thanksgiving*

December
31st – *New Year's* _____ *party*

2 Now make your own calendar. Note important dates and plans in your year.

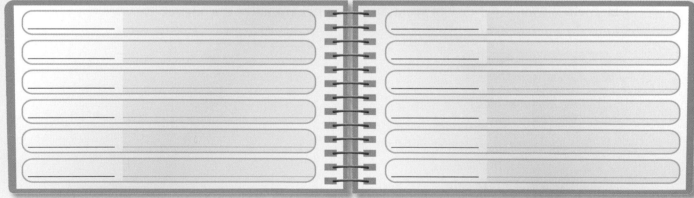

On your own

Buy a wall calendar. Circle your important dates, and write the things you are going to do in English. Put it on the wall so you can see it.

Growing up

In Unit 5, you learn how to . . .

- use the simple past in statements and questions (review).
- use time expressions to talk about the past.
- use *all*, *most*, *a lot of*, *a few*, etc.
- talk about memories of childhood, school, and your teenage years.
- correct yourself with expressions like *Wait*, *Actually*, and *I mean*.

1

2

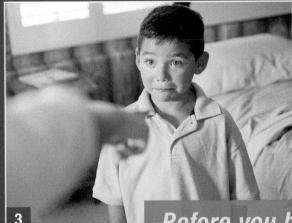

3

4

Before you begin . . .

Do you remember . . . Do you have memories like these? Do you remember . . .

- sleepovers with your friends?
- a time you got into trouble?
- learning to swim?
- your first close friend?

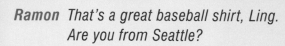

Childhood

Ramon	That's a great baseball shirt, Ling. Are you from Seattle?
Ling	Um, kind of. I lived there, but I wasn't born there.
Ramon	Oh, yeah? Where were you born?
Ling	In São Paulo, actually.
Ramon	São Paulo? Brazil?
Ling	Yeah. My parents were born in Hong Kong, but they moved to São Paulo in 1986, just before I was born.
Ramon	Wow. How long did you live there?
Ling	Until I was six. Then we moved to the U.S.
Ramon	To Seattle?
Ling	Yeah. We lived there for ten years, and we came here to San Francisco about three years ago.
Ramon	Huh. So did you grow up bilingual?
Ling	Well, we always spoke Chinese at home. I couldn't speak English until I went to school. And actually, I can still speak a little Portuguese.

Getting started

A Listen. Where was Ling born? Where does she live now? Practice the conversation.

> **Figure it out**

B Can you complete the sentences? Use the conversation above to help you.

1. Ling's family left Hong Kong _____ 1986.
2. Ling lived in São Paulo _____ six years.
3. Her family stayed there _____ she was six.
4. They moved to Seattle. _____ they came to San Francisco.
5. They moved to San Francisco three years _____ .

2 Grammar be born; simple past (review); time expressions

Where **were** you **born**? I **was born** in São Paulo. I **wasn't born** in Seattle.	Where **were** your parents **born**? They **were born** in Hong Kong. They **weren't born** in the U.S.
Did you live there **for a long time**? Yes, (I did). I lived there **for six years**. No, (I didn't). I didn't live there **long**.	How long did you live in São Paulo? We lived there **until** I was six. **From** 1986 **to** 1992. We didn't leave **until** 1992. **Then** we came to the U.S.
Did she move here **last year**? Yes, (she did). She moved **in May**. No, (she didn't). She moved **in 2002**.	When did they come here? They came here about **three years ago**. They came **when** Ling was sixteen.

About you

A Complete the sentences with time expressions so they are true for you. Then compare with a partner.

> **Saying years**
>
> 1906 = "Nineteen oh-six"
> 1988 = "Nineteen eighty-eight"
> 2007 = "Two thousand (and) seven"
> 2015 = "Twenty fifteen"

1. I learned to ride a bicycle in __1988__ , when __I was seven__ .
2. My best friend was born _____ ago, in _____ .
3. I played a musical instrument for _____ ,
   until _____ .
4. I went to elementary school until _____ ,
   from _____ to _____ .
5. My family last went on vacation together in _____ , when _____ .

B Complete the questions. Then ask and answer the questions with a partner.

1. Where _____ your mother born?
   _____ your father born there, too?

2. Where _____ you grow up?
   _____ you born there?

3. Who _____ your best friend in school?
   How long _____ you best friends?

4. _____ you and your best friend ever fight?
   _____ you ever get in trouble?

5. Who took care of you when you _____ little?
   _____ your mother have a job?

3 Speaking naturally did you

Where **did you** go on vacation?	What **did you** do?	**Did you** have fun?

A Listen and repeat the questions above. Notice the ways of saying *did you*.

About you

B Listen and complete the questions about your childhood vacations. Then ask and answer the questions with a partner.

When you were a child, . . .
1. Did you _____ ?
2. Where did you _____ ?
3. Who did you _____ ?
4. How long did you _____ ?
5. Did you _____ ?
6. What did you _____ ?

1 Building language

A  Listen. What languages did these people study in school?

What languages did you learn in school?

Keiko

All the students in my high school had to take English – it was required. And I needed English to get into my university. (Tokyo)

Mirka

Well, years ago, most people learned Russian and only a few people took English. I studied both. (Warsaw)

Brad

I took Spanish last year, and most of my friends did, too. There are a lot of Spanish speakers around here, so it's kind of useful. (Los Angeles)

Paul

A lot of my classmates dropped French after ninth grade. Almost all of them – except me. But then later, some of them had to take evening classes because they needed it for work. (Lagos)

Figure it out

B Circle the correct expression to complete these sentences. Are they true for you?

1. **Most / Most of** my friends are fluent in English.   2. **A few / A few of** people in my city know Russian.

2 Grammar Determiners

General		Specific			
All	**children** learn a language.	**All (of)**	**the children in my town** take English.	**All of**	**them . . .**
Most	**Canadians** need French.	**Most of**	**the people in my office** know French.	**Most of**	**us . . .**
Some	**students** take Spanish.	**Some of**	**the students in my class** take Greek.	**Some of**	**us . . .**
A few	**people** are good at Latin.	**A few of**	**my classmates** got As.	**A few of**	**them . . .**
No	**students** like exams.	**None of**	**my friends** failed the exams.	**None of**	**them . . .**
But:					
A lot of	**people** speak English well.	**A lot of**	**the people in this city** speak English.	**A lot of**	**them . . .**

About you

Make true sentences using determiners. Compare with a partner.

1. _____ my friends studied English in junior high school.
   _____ junior high school students take English.
2. Today _____ employees need a second language for their jobs.
   _____ my friends speak two languages.
3. _____ college students major in languages.
   _____ the colleges here teach several different languages.
4. _____ students take two languages in high school.
   In my class, _____ us studied two languages.

In conversation . . .

People usually say **everybody** and **nobody**, not **all people** or **no people**.

3 Building vocabulary

A Listen and say the subjects. Can you think of other subjects and categories? Which subjects are you interested in? Tell the class.

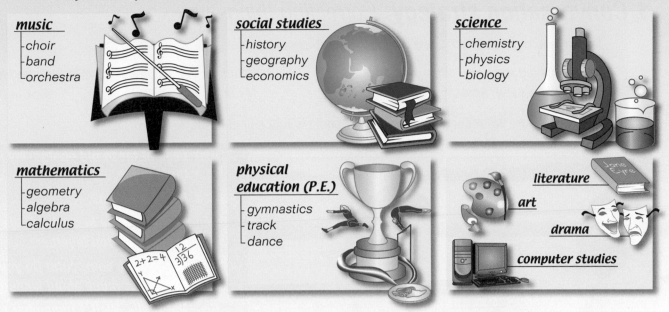

music
- choir
- band
- orchestra

social studies
- history
- geography
- economics

science
- chemistry
- physics
- biology

mathematics
- geometry
- algebra
- calculus

physical education (P.E.)
- gymnastics
- track
- dance

literature

art

drama

computer studies

Word sort → **B** Complete the chart with different subjects. Then compare with a partner.

I like / liked . . .	I don't like / didn't like . . .	I'd like to study . . .
algebra	geography	

4 Survey *What were your best subjects?*

A *Class activity* Complete the questions with different subjects. Then ask your classmates the questions. Keep a tally of the answers. If you are still in high school, talk about last year.

	Yes	No
Did you study ___chemistry___ ?	ℍℍ	II
Were you good at _____ ?		
Did you get good grades in _____ ?		

	Yes	No
Were your _____ classes hard ?		
Did you enjoy _____ ?		
Did you hate _____ ?		

B Tell the class your results. What interesting information do you learn?

"Most of us studied chemistry. Only a few people were good at physics. . . ."

5 Vocabulary notebook *I hated math!*

See page 52 for a new way to log and learn vocabulary.

Well, actually, . . .

1 Conversation strategy Correcting things you say

A Can you think of possible ways to complete these replies?

A How old were you when you moved here?

B I was seven. Actually, no, I was _____ .

A Who took you to school on your first day?

B My mom. No, wait, my _____ took me.

Now listen. What does Ben remember about his first day of school?

Ben Look at these old photos. My mom sent them to me.

Jessica Oh, is this you?

Ben Yeah, with my best friend. We were in kindergarten together.

Jessica Oh, . . . you were cute! Do you remember much about kindergarten?

Ben Not really. Well, I remember my first day of school. Actually, I don't remember the day, but I remember on the way home I missed my bus stop.

Jessica Oh, no!

Ben Yeah. And I kept riding around until I was the last kid on the bus.

Jessica So how did you get home?

Ben Well, the teacher, I mean, the bus driver, had to call and find out my address and everything, and he took me home.

Jessica So that was when you were five?

Ben Yeah. Uh . . . no, wait. . . . I was only four. I started school early.

Notice how Ben corrects the things he says with expressions like these: *Well*; *Actually*; *No, wait*. Find examples in the conversation.

"No, wait. . . . I was only four."

B Match the sentences with the corrections. Then compare with a partner.

1. I don't remember anything about my childhood. *e*
2. I started gymnastics when I was five. _____
3. I hated swimming lessons. _____
4. I lived with my grandparents for a year. _____
5. I played piano until I was ten. _____
6. All my friends were very nice. _____

a. Actually, no, I was 11 when I quit.
b. Well, they were OK, but I was always scared
c. Well, most of them, not all of them.
d. No, wait. I was six.
e. Well, actually, I remember a few things.
f. No, wait. Actually, it was two years.

About you → **C** *Pair work* Tell a partner three things about your childhood, but make a few mistakes. Correct the information with *Well*; *Actually*; or *No, wait*.

SELF-STUDY
AUDIO CD
CD-ROM

2 Strategy plus *I mean*

You can use *I mean* to correct yourself when you say the wrong word or name. This is just one use of *I mean*.

Well, the teacher, I mean, the bus driver, had to . . .

A Complete the questions by correcting the underlined words. Use the words on the right.

In conversation . . .

Mean is one of the top 100 words. About 90% of its uses are in the expression *I mean*.

When you were a child, . . .

1. Did you read a lot of <u>cartoons</u>, I mean, <u>comic books</u> ?
2. Did you have a <u>motorbike</u>, I mean, a _____ ?
3. How often did you visit your <u>parents</u>, I mean, your _____ ?
4. Did you go <u>skiing</u> in the winter, I mean, _____ ?
5. Were you afraid of <u>cats</u>, I mean, _____ ?
6. Did you have an imaginary <u>classmate</u>, I mean, _____ ?
7. Did you collect <u>animals</u>, I mean, _____ ?
8. Were you good at playing <u>chess</u>, I mean, _____ ?

stuffed animals
checkers
friend
mountain bike
skating
✓ **comic books**
dogs
grandparents

 B *Pair work* Ask and answer the questions. Continue your conversations.

"Did you read a lot of cartoons, I mean, comic books?"   *"Yes, I did. My favorite was . . ."*

3 Listening and speaking *I don't remember exactly . . .*

A Listen to people talk about their childhood memories. Underline the words they correct. Write the corrections on the lines.

1. When I was <u>three</u>, we moved to another city for a few years. <u>four</u>
2. I played softball until I was in sixth grade, and then I got interested in other sports, like football. _____
3. My mother made clothes for me and my brother. One time, she made me some dark blue shorts. They were awful. _____
4. I met my best friend in 1996. We were in high school together. _____
5. All the kids teased me in school because I had an unusual name. But one kid was really nice to me. _____

B *Pair work* Take turns telling memories of growing up. Ask questions to find out more information.

"I got into trouble one time."   *"Oh? What did you do?"*

4 Free talk *In the past*

See *Free talk 5* for more speaking practice.

Teenage years

1 Reading

A Brainstorm the word *teenager*! What do you think of? Make a class list.

> teenager: parties, loud music, fights with parents

B Read the interview. Which of Jennifer's answers are funny? Which are interesting?

AN **INTERVIEW** WITH . . .
Jennifer Wilkin

Jennifer works in publishing. We asked her about her memories of being a teenager.

Did you enjoy being a teenager?
It was mostly OK, but I had some difficulties, like everyone else. When you're a teenager, you're unsure of yourself.

What were the fashions then?
I was a teenager in the '80s, and so the clothes were very colorful. I was a fashion rebel, though – I always wore black, and I wore a lot of cheap silver jewelry. Often I wore vintage clothing.

What kind of music did you listen to?
My tastes were varied – I was a classical violinist, but I listened to punk rock and new wave music. I had all my "weird" cassette tapes, and I was never without them.

What's your best memory from your teenage years?
I guess it was a trip I took every summer with my youth group. It was a time to travel, be with close friends, and be away from my parents.

And your worst?
I think going to school was the worst. I'm not a social type, and it gave me all kinds of anxiety.

What's one thing you remember about school?
I remember that everybody tried to be different, but they tried to be the same, also.

What was your favorite subject?
My favorite subject was psychology. I loved analyzing my friends.

Were you ever in trouble? Why?
I got detention lots of times because I was late for school every morning, but I never got in real trouble.

How did you spend your free time?
Actually, I spent a lot of time driving around in friends' cars, honking at people's houses as we drove by. I also spent time reading, playing with my dog and cat, or tormenting my younger sister.

What do you miss about your teenage days?
NOTHING! Except my jeans size.

What's one piece of advice you would give to today's teenagers?
Get off your computer, and turn off the TV!

C Add these missing sentences to the interview with Jennifer. Write the numbers in the spaces.

1 I have no idea now why we did that!

2 I was always happy to get home, though.

3 I tried my best to look different.

4 I hardly ever listened to the radio.

5 And you're always trying to fit in.

2 Listening *A long time ago*

Listen to Colin talk about being a teenager in England many years ago. Complete the sentences by circling *a*, *b*, or *c*.

1. Colin was a teenager	a. in the '40s.	b. in the '50s.	c. in the '60s.
2. He quit school when he was	a. 13.	b. 14.	c. 15.
3. His first job was	a. in a factory.	b. in a store.	c. on a farm.
4. His main interest was	a. music.	b. buying clothes.	c. watching TV.
5. His main regret is that he	a. spent a lot of money.	b. didn't take classes.	c. didn't have fun.

3 Writing *An interview*

A Write five interview questions to ask a classmate about when he or she was younger. Leave spaces for the answers.

> 1. Did you get along with your parents?
>
> 2. Were you a good student?

B Exchange your questions with a classmate. Write answers to your classmate's questions.

> 1. Did you get along with your parents?
> Yes, I did. I was busy, so I didn't see them much. We agreed on most things except for the car. We had a lot of fights about that.

> **Help note**
>
> **Linking ideas:** *except (for), apart from*
> We agreed on most things **except for** the car.
> We didn't agree on much **apart from** my best friend. They liked her.

C *Pair work* Now read your partner's answers. Ask questions to find out more information.

Vocabulary notebook

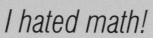 *I hated math!*

Learning tip *Grouping vocabulary*

You can group new vocabulary in different ways to help you remember it. For example, group things you can or can't do, or things you are interested in or not interested in.

Talk about school

The top 4 school subjects people talk about are:

1. math   3. physics
2. science   4. history

People say *math* almost 10 times more than *mathematics*.

1 Complete the chart with these school subjects.

biology	chemistry	English	geography	history
math	physics	P.E.	art	music

I'm / I was good at . . .	*I'm not / I wasn't very good at . . .*	*I can't / I couldn't do . . . at all.*

2 Now complete this chart. Use the school subjects above, and add more.

I like / liked . . .	*I hate / hated . . .*	*I'm not / I wasn't really interested in . . .*

On your own

Walk around a large bookstore, and look at the different sections. How many subjects do you know in English?

Around town

In Unit 6, you learn how to . . .

- use *Is there?* and *Are there?* to ask about places in a town.
- use location expressions like *across from* and *outside*.
- use *Can* and *Could* to offer help and ask for directions.
- talk about stores and favorite places in your city or town.
- check information by repeating key words, using "checking" expressions and asking "echo" questions.

3

1

2

4

Before you begin . . .

Match each comment with a picture.

☐ "There's a lot to see." ☐ "It's great for shopping."

☐ "It's easy to get around." ☐ "There's a lot of nightlife."

What else can you say about each place?

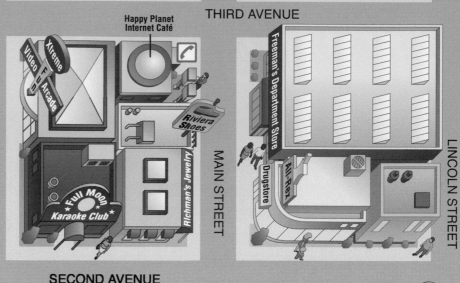

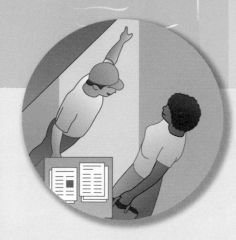

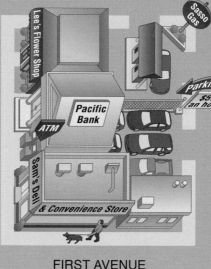

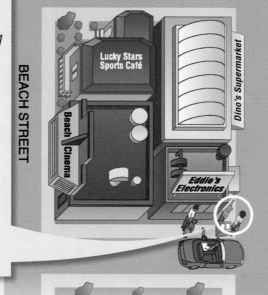

THIRD AVENUE

Happy Planet Internet Café

MAIN STREET

LINCOLN STREET

SECOND AVENUE

BEACH STREET

FIRST AVENUE

Woman Excuse me, please. Is there an Internet café near here?

Jack Uh . . . there's one on Main Street – across from the big department store. It's right up this street.

Woman Thanks. Oh, and are there any cash machines around here?

Jack Yeah. There are some ATMs over there outside the bank, just across the street.

Woman Oh, yeah. I see them. Thanks.

1 Getting started

A How often do you go to places like the ones above? What can you do or buy in these places? Tell the class.

B 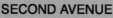 Listen. A woman is asking Jack for help. What is she looking for? Practice the conversation.

Figure it out → **C** Can you complete these questions and answers? Practice with a partner.

❶ *Boy* __Is there__ a video arcade near here?

   Jack Yes, there's _____ on Beach Street.

❷ *Man* _____ any pay phones around here?

   Jack Yes, there are _____ in front of the Happy Planet Internet Café.

2 Grammar *Is there? Are there?; location expressions* 🔊

Is there an Internet café near here?
   Yes, there is. There's **one** on Main Street.
   It's across from the department store.
   No, there isn't **(one)**.

Are there any cash machines near here?
   Yes, there are. There are **some** outside the bank.
   Yes, there's **one** over there.
   No, there aren't **(any)**.

A Look at the map on page 54. Complete the questions with *Is there a* or *Are there any*. Complete the answers with *one, some, any,* and location expressions. Then practice with a partner.

Driver <u>Is there a</u> bank around here?

Jack Yeah, there's <u>one</u> right <u>on</u> Main Street.
   It's _____ the deli. Do you see Sam's Deli –
   just _____ the street?

Driver Oh, yeah. Can I park there? I mean, _____
   parking lot?

Jack Well, there's _____ just _____ the
   bank, but the entrance is _____ Lincoln.

Driver _____ public restrooms there?

Jack No, there aren't _____ . But there's a
   department store _____ Main and Third. I'm
   sure there are _____ there, _____
   the store.

Driver Thanks. Oh, and _____ supermarket anywhere?

Jack Uh, there's _____ over there – _____
   the bank.

Driver And one more thing – _____ shoe stores near here?

Jack Yes, there's Riviera Shoes on Main, _____
   Second and Third Avenues.

Location expressions

behind

in front of

next to

between

inside

outside

on First Street

on the corner of Main and First

across (the street) from opposite

B *Pair work* Now ask and answer questions about these places on the map.

   a jewelry store   **restaurants**   **a karaoke club**   **gas stations**   **an electronics store**

3 Speaking naturally *Word stress in compound nouns*

  ● ●   ● ●   ● ●
bookstore   *restroom*   *pay phone*

A 🔊 Listen and repeat the compound nouns above. Notice the stress pattern.

B 🔊 Listen and complete the questions. Then ask and answer the questions with a partner.

1. Are there any good _____ near your home?
2. Is there a big _____ around here?
3. Are there any _____ outside this building?
4. Is there a _____ in this neighborhood?
5. Is there a good _____ near your home?
6. Are there any _____ around here?

Getting around

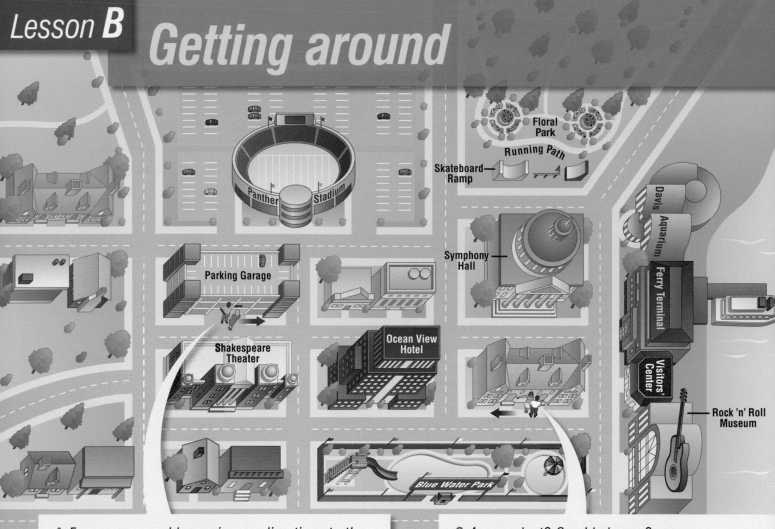

Panther Stadium

Floral Park

Running Path

Skateboard Ramp

Symphony Hall

Davis Aquarium

Ferry Terminal

Parking Garage

Ocean View Hotel

Visitors' Center

Shakespeare Theater

Rock 'n' Roll Museum

Blue Water Park

A *Excuse me, could you give me directions to the Rock 'n' Roll Museum?*

B *Sure. Go straight ahead for two blocks. You're going to see a ferry terminal. Make a right and go down the street about a block. It's on the left.*

C *Are you lost? Can I help you?*

D *Yes, thanks. Can you tell me how to get to Panther Stadium?*

C *Sure. Go to the end of the next block, and turn right. Walk up two blocks. You can't miss it.*

1 Building vocabulary

A 💿 Listen to the conversations, and follow the directions on the map. Then underline all the expressions for directions. Practice with a partner.

Figure it out ▶ **B** Can you put these directions in order? First find your location on the map, and then find your destination.

You're just outside the parking garage. You ask:
"Could you tell me how to get to the aquarium?"

☐	*The aquarium is going to be on your right.*
☐	*You're going to see a ferry terminal.*
1	*Go straight ahead for two blocks.*
☐	*Make a left.*
☐	*Walk up the street about one block.*

You're in the Ocean View Hotel. You ask:
"Can you give me directions to Symphony Hall?"

☐	*Then make a right.*
☐	*Turn left again at the corner, and walk up a block.*
☐	*It's right there, on the left.*
☐	*When you go out of the hotel, turn left.*

2 Grammar *Offers and requests with Can and Could*

Offers	Requests
Can I help you?	**Can** you help me?
What **can** I do?	**Can** you tell me how to get to the aquarium?
How **can** I help?	**Could** you give me directions?

In conversation . . .

Can you . . . ? is more common than *Could you . . . ?* for requests. People use *Could you . . . ?* to make their requests more polite.

Can you . . . ?

Could you . . . ?

A Some people are asking for directions at the Visitors' Center on the map on page 56. Complete the questions and write directions for each person.

1. *A* _____ you tell me how to get to Panther Stadium?
   B Sure. Just go _____ .

2. *A* _____ you give me directions to the Shakespeare Theater? Is it far from here?
   B Uh, it's not far. Walk _____ .

3. *A* _____ you recommend a place to go running?
   B Let me think. There's a running path in Floral Park. Go _____ .

4. *A* _____ I help you?
   B Yes, thanks. Is this the right way to Blue Water Park?
   A Yes, just go _____ .

B *Pair work* Now take turns asking for and giving directions to the places above.

3 Listening and speaking *Finding your way around*

A Look at the map on page 56. Listen to the concierge at the Ocean View Hotel give directions to people. Where do they want to go? Number the places.

☐ **the aquarium** ☐ **the ferry terminal** ☐ **the Rock 'n' Roll Museum** ☐ **Panther Stadium**

B *Pair work* Ask and answer questions about the neighborhood you are in. Use these questions, or think of your own.

▶ Could you recommend a cheap restaurant around here?
▶ Is there a place to go skateboarding or biking near here?
▶ Can you tell me how to get to the subway or to a bus stop?
▶ Could you give me directions to the nearest video arcade?

A **Could you recommend a cheap restaurant around here?**
B **Sure. Try Ann's Diner. When you leave the building, turn left. Then . . .**

4 Vocabulary notebook *Which way?*

See page 62 for a new way to log and learn vocabulary.

Excuse me?

Conversation strategy *Checking information*

A What are the best ways to check information? Choose two responses.

A Excuse me. Is there a mall around here?
B ☐ Huh?   ☐ A mall?   ☐ Did you say a mall?

Now listen. What is there to do near the hotel?

Restaurant ↑
Meeting Rooms
← Parking

CONCIERGE

Concierge	Hi. Can I help you?
Kate	Yes. What is there to do around here? Within walking distance.
Concierge	Within walking distance? Well, the Center Mall is a 15-minute walk from here.
Kate	Fifteen or fifty?
Concierge	Fifteen. They have a lot of good stores and movie theaters. Or if you want to go see a play, there's . . .
Kate	I'm sorry? A play? Um . . . no, I think a movie sounds better. Did you say the Center Mall?
Concierge	Yes, it's right down this street. The new John Woo movie is playing – I heard it's good.
Kate	Excuse me? The new what?
Concierge	The new John Woo movie. It got great reviews.

Notice how Kate and the concierge check information. They repeat words as a question or use "checking" expressions. Find examples in the conversation.

"It's a 15-minute walk from here."
"Fifteen or fifty?"

"Checking" expressions
I'm sorry?
Excuse me?
Did you say . . . ?
What did you say?

B Match the questions with the checking responses. Then practice with a partner. Give your own answers.

1. Could you give me directions to the airport? __c__
2. Is there an Indonesian restaurant near here? _____
3. Do you have a number for a cab company? _____
4. Where is there a bookstore around here? _____
5. Are there any good concerts on this week? _____

a. Did you say Indian or Indonesian?
b. I'm sorry? Did you say a bookstore?
c. Sorry, what did you say? The airport?
d. Excuse me? Did you say cab?
e. Concerts, did you say?

SELF-STUDY
AUDIO CD
CD-ROM

2 Strategy plus *"Echo" questions*

In an "echo" question, you repeat something you heard, and you add a question word to check information you didn't hear.

The new John Woo movie is playing.

Excuse me? The new what?

Here are some more examples:
A *The video arcade is on Beach Street.*
B *I'm sorry, it's where?*

A *It opens at 10:00.*
B *Excuse me? It opens at what time?*

> ▶ **In conversation . . .**

When people ask others to repeat information, they say **I'm sorry?** more often than **Excuse me?**

▮▮▮▮▮ **I'm sorry?**

▮▮▮ **Excuse me?**

A Complete the conversations with "echo" questions. Use the question words in the box. Then practice with a partner.

how far	how much	✓what	what kind	what time	where

1. *A* There are lots of street performers in the city right now.
   B I'm sorry, there are a lot of ____**what**____ ?
2. *A* There's a miniature golf course about 15 minutes away.
   B Excuse me, it's _____ ?
3. *A* The best outdoor pool around here is at Ocean Beach.
   B I'm sorry, it's _____ ?
4. *A* There are great gift shops in this neighborhood.
   B I'm sorry, there are _____ of shops?
5. *A* The movie theater opens at 10:15 a.m.
   B Excuse me, it opens at _____ ?
6. *A* Rides in the amusement park cost $5.
   B They cost _____ ?

> **About you**

B *Pair work* Student A: Tell a partner about a place you know well. Use the ideas above. Student B: Check the information you hear. Then change roles.

"There are some nice stores in this neighborhood."   *"I'm sorry, there are some what?"*

3 Listening *Tourist information*

A 💿 Listen to the beginning of six conversations at a tourist-information desk. What do you think each person says next to check the information? Number the sentences.

☐ *"Excuse me? Thirteen or thirty?"*	1 *"Did you say Greek?"*	☐ *"I'm sorry? What time?"*
☐ *"Cookies and what, did you say?"*	☐ *"I'm sorry, any what? Concerts?"*	☐ *"Did you say bicycles?"*

B 💿 Now listen to the complete conversations, and check your answers. What other information does the clerk give each person? Make notes. Then compare with a partner.

59

1 Reading

A Are there any interesting places to walk around your city? Where are they?
Can you go on a walking tour? Tell the class.

B Read these pages from a walking-tour guide. As you read, follow the tour on the map.

A Walking Tour of San Francisco's
CHINATOWN

San Francisco's Chinatown is the largest Chinese community on the West Coast of the U.S. and is now home to over 14,000 people. Chinese settlers came here as early as 1846, opening businesses near Portsmouth Square.

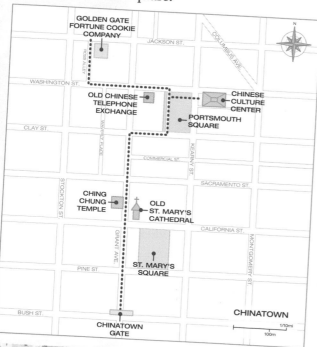

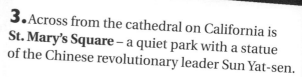

3. Across from the cathedral on California is **St. Mary's Square** – a quiet park with a statue of the Chinese revolutionary leader Sun Yat-sen.

4. Opposite the cathedral on Grant, the **Ching Chung Temple** welcomes visitors and has year-round guided tours.

5. Continue north on Grant, and turn right on Clay Street. Then turn left into **Portsmouth Square**, and watch local people play cards or Chinese chess.

6. Take the footbridge across Kearny Street to the **Chinese Culture Center**. Here there are exhibitions of Chinese and Chinese-American art, as well as a permanent display of Chinese musical instruments. It's well worth a visit.

7. Return to the square, and turn left onto Washington Street. On the left is the **Old Chinese Telephone Exchange**. Now a bank, the exchange opened in 1909. Operators had to speak English and five Chinese dialects.

I. The tour begins at the **Chinatown Gate** at the intersection of Bush Street and Grant Avenue. Walk north on Grant – a busy street of shops selling souvenirs, jewelry, artwork, furniture, cameras, and electronics.

2. At the corner of California and Grant, look around **Old St. Mary's Cathedral** (1891) and its display of historic photographs of 19th-century Chinatown.

8. Continue west on Washington, and turn right into Ross Alley. Near the end of the block is the **Golden Gate Fortune Cookie Company**, where you can sample the fortune cookies.

This is where your tour ends. We hope you enjoy your tour of San Francisco's Chinatown.

C Read the guide again, and answer the questions. Then compare with a partner.

1. Where can you do these things, according to the guide?
   a. look at old photographs
   b. listen to someone talk about a temple
   c. buy Chinese art
   d. eat a well-known dessert
2. Where is the best place to take interesting pictures, do you think?
3. Which three places would you like to see on this tour? Why?

2 *Talk about it* *What are some of your favorite places?*

Group work Discuss places in your town or city.
Can you agree on the best place to do these things?

Is there . . .
► a good place to sit and watch people go by?
► a fun place to spend a rainy afternoon?
► a cheap (but good) place to eat?
► a quiet area to go for a walk or a jog?
► a good place to shop for electronic products?
► an interesting museum?
► a neighborhood with lots of cultural events?
► a neighborhood with lots of interesting nightlife?

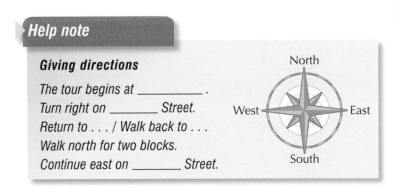

3 *Writing* *A walking-tour guide*

A Write a guide for a walking tour for an area in your city or town. Write about three different places. Give directions and explain why they are worth a visit.

Document 1

A Walking Tour of Rockville

The tour begins at Monterey Park. It's a beautiful park with a big lake. It has beautiful flower gardens all year.

Enter the park on Lincoln Avenue. Walk along the road until you get to the lake. Find a nice park bench. It's a good place to sit and watch people.

Walk back to the entrance, and turn right on Lincoln Avenue. . . .

Help note

Giving directions
The tour begins at _____ .
Turn right on _____ *Street.*
Return to . . . / Walk back to . . .
Walk north for two blocks.
Continue east on _____ *Street.*

B *Group work* Read your classmates' guides. Choose a tour you would like to take. Tell the group which tour you chose and why.

4 *Free talk* *Summer fun*

For more speaking practice, go to the back of the book.
Student A: See *Free talk 6A*. Student B: See *Free talk 6B*.

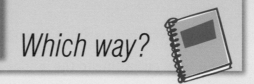

Which way?

Learning tip *Drawing maps*

Draw and label a map to help you remember directions.

People say **around here** 50 times more frequently than **near here**.

1 Use the map to number the directions to the bank below.

Directions

☐	Walk one more block.
☐	Turn right.
1	Walk up one block.
☐	Make a left.
☐	It's on the left, just past the post office.

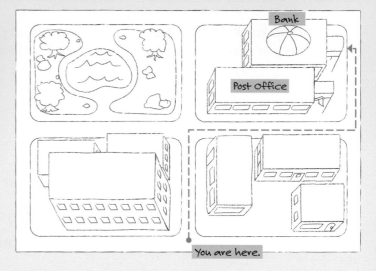

2 Now draw your own map. Show the way from your home or class to a place you often go to. Then write the directions to go with the map.

Directions from my _____ to _____

1. _____
   _____

2. _____
   _____

3. _____
   _____

4. _____
   _____

My map

On your own

Find a map of your town or city. Highlight the route from one place you know to another. Then write directions. Learn the directions.

1 Unscramble the questions.

Put the words in the correct order to make questions. Then ask and answer the questions with a partner.

1. doing / are / next weekend / what / you ?

   <u>What are you doing next weekend?</u>

2. after class / going to / you / go shopping / are ?

   _____

3. it / rain / tomorrow / going to / is ?

   _____

4. you / here / did / another city / from / move ?

   _____

5. last year / you / did / on vacation / go / where ?

   _____

6. what / your / in school / favorite / was / subject ?

   _____

7. arc / a lot of / in / fun places / neighborhood / there / your ?

   _____

2 Can you complete this conversation?

Complete the conversation. Use the words and expressions in the box. Use capital letters where necesssary. Then practice with a partner.

where	✓is there a	I mean	was born	until		did you say	I'm not sure
what	him	and everything	one		my grandfather	actually	

A <u>Is there a</u> good music store around here?

B There's _____ on the corner of Fifth and Oak.

A It's _____ ?

B On Fifth Avenue, _____ , Sixth Avenue, and Oak.

A _____ Sixth Avenue? A couple of blocks away?

B Yeah. They have all kinds of music, and you can watch music videos and do karaoke _____ .

A You can do _____ ?

B Karaoke. I went last week. Well, _____ , I didn't go inside, but it looks great. Do you want to go?

A Now? _____ . What time does it close?

B It doesn't close _____ midnight.

A Oh, OK. I can get _____ a video for his birthday.

B You buy _____ music videos? How old is he?

A Well, he _____ in 1945, so how old is that?

B I don't know. I never could do math.

3 *What can you remember?*

A Add five words to each category, and compare with a partner. Ask questions to find out more information.

"Are you going to celebrate Halloween?"   *"Yes, I am. You too? Are you going to have a party, or . . . ?"*

Events you are going to celebrate this year	Important dates for you	Places in town you go to often	Subjects you're never going to study
Halloween	May 1st – my birthday	the bank	biology

B Choose a category and survey your class or group. Report your findings to the class.

"Most of us are going to celebrate Halloween."   *"Nobody is going to send a Valentine's card."*

4 *Get it right!*

A Can you complete these questions? Use the words in the box.

walk
best
neighborhood
weddings
cash machine

1. What's your city, I mean, your _____ like?
2. Are you going to any birthday parties, I mean, _____ this year?
3. Can you give me directions to a bank around here? I mean, a _____ ?
4. When did you learn to swim? I mean, when did you learn to _____ ?
5. What was your worst, I mean, _____ subject in school?

B *Pair work* Take turns asking the questions. Use "vague" expressions in your answers. Check your partner's answers with "echo" questions.

A What's your city, I mean, your neighborhood like?
B Well, I like it. There's a lot to do. We have a lot of cafés and restaurants and everything.
A I'm sorry. A lot of what?

5 *Do you know your city?*

Pair work Write directions from your school to three places nearby. Then trade papers. Can your partner guess the places?

1. Cross the street, turn left, and walk up three blocks. This place is on the right, next to the bank. What is it?

1. The music store.

Self-check

How sure are you about these areas?
Circle the percentages.

grammar
20% 40% 60% 80% 100%
vocabulary
20% 40% 60% 80% 100%
conversation strategies
20% 40% 60% 80% 100%

. . . .

Study plan

What do you want to review?
Circle the lessons.

grammar
4A 4B 5A 5B 6A 6B
vocabulary
4A 4B 5A 5B 6A 6B
conversation strategies
4C 5C 6C

Going away

In Unit 7, you learn how to . . .
- use infinitives to give reasons.
- use *it* in sentences like *It's easy to do*.
- ask for and give advice and suggestions.
- talk about vacations and getting ready for a trip.
- respond to suggestions.
- use *I guess* to sound less sure about something.

Before you begin . . .
Brainstorm! Think of three . . .
- fun places to go on a trip.
- different ways to travel.
- things you always take on a trip.
- fun things to do on a trip.

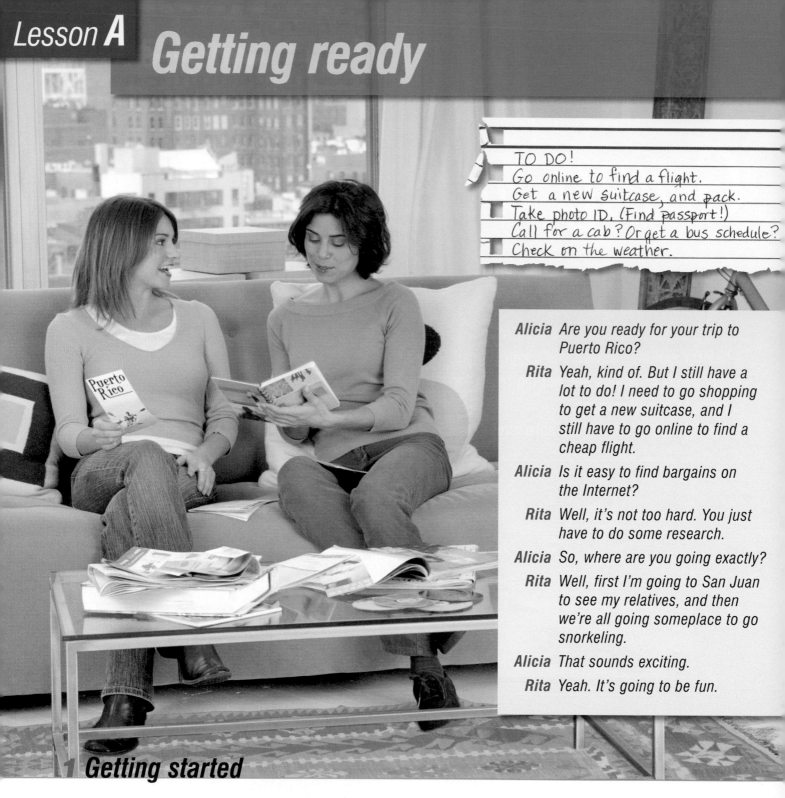

> **TO DO!**
> Go online to find a flight.
> Get a new suitcase, and pack.
> Take photo ID. (Find passport!)
> Call for a cab? Or get a bus schedule?
> Check on the weather.

Alicia Are you ready for your trip to Puerto Rico?

Rita Yeah, kind of. But I still have a lot to do! I need to go shopping to get a new suitcase, and I still have to go online to find a cheap flight.

Alicia Is it easy to find bargains on the Internet?

Rita Well, it's not too hard. You just have to do some research.

Alicia So, where are you going exactly?

Rita Well, first I'm going to San Juan to see my relatives, and then we're all going someplace to go snorkeling.

Alicia That sounds exciting.

Rita Yeah. It's going to be fun.

1 Getting started

A Look at Rita's "to do" list for her upcoming trip. What other things do you need to do before a trip? Make a class list.

B 🔊 Listen. What is Rita going to do on her trip? Practice the conversation.

Figure it out **C** Can you complete the sentences? Use the conversation above to help you.

1. Rita's planning a trip to Puerto Rico _____ her relatives.
2. Rita still has to go on the Internet _____ some research on cheap flights.
3. It's not hard _____ bargains online.

2 Grammar *Infinitives for reasons; It's + adjective + to . . .*

I'm going to Puerto Rico **to see** my relatives.   **Is it** easy **to find** bargains online?
I need to go shopping **to get** a suitcase.   **It's** easy **to do**.
I have to go online **to find** a flight.   **It's** not hard **to do**.

A Imagine you are planning a trip to a foreign country. Make sentences about things you have to do. Then match each sentence with a question someone might ask you.

> ***In conversation . . .***
>
> The top five adjectives in the structure *It's _____ to . . .* are *hard*, *nice*, *easy*, *good*, and *important*.

> 1. I need to get a phrase book to learn some expressions.

1. get a phrase book / learn some expressions __e__
2. call the embassy / ask about a visa _____
3. go on the Internet / get a flight _____
4. call a travel agent / get a hotel room _____
5. buy a guidebook / find out about trains _____
6. go to the bank / change some money _____

a. Is it hard to get a visa?
b. Is it safe to pay online with a credit card?
c. Is it easy to get around?
d. Is it safe to carry a lot of cash?
e. Is it necessary to know the language?
f. Is it good to make reservations in advance?

B *Pair work* Choose a country to visit. Role-play a conversation about getting ready for a trip there. Use your sentences and the questions above for ideas.

A *I'm going to Brazil, so I need to get a phrase book to learn some Portuguese.*
B *Is it necessary to know Portuguese?*
A *Well, I think it's nice to say **hello** and **thank you** and things like that.*

3 Speaking naturally *Reduction of to*

*Is it expensive **to** visit your country?*   *Well, it's hard **to** find cheap hotels.*

A Listen and repeat. Notice the reduction of *to* in the sentences above.

B Listen to questions from two people who are planning to visit your country. Complete their questions.

1. Do you need to speak the language _____ ?
2. Is it OK _____ ?
3. Do you have _____ with you all the time?
4. Is it safe _____ late at night?
5. Can you use a credit card _____ in restaurants?

About you

C *Group work* Discuss the questions above. Do you all agree?

A *Well, you don't need to speak Spanish in the big cities.*
B *Yeah, but it's good to know some if you go to small towns.*

1 Building vocabulary

A 🔘 Listen and say the words. Which items are good to take on a beach vacation? Circle ten things. Then compare with a partner.

a tent

a towel

a bathing suit

a sleeping bag

insect repellent

a first-aid kit

sandals

makeup

a pair of scissors

shampoo

a brush

sunscreen

a flashlight

toothpaste

a toothbrush

pajamas

batteries

a hair dryer

soap

a razor

Word
sort

B Think of three things you need and three things you don't need to take on these trips. Complete the chart. Then compare with a partner.

	On a camping trip	On a business trip	To stay overnight with a friend
You need	a tent		
You don't need	a hair dryer		

"On a camping trip, you need to take a tent."   "Yeah, and it's important to have . . ."

2 Building language

A  Listen. Jenny's going on a camping trip. What's her mother's advice? Practice the conversation.

Mom Jenny, maybe you should take some insect repellent. . . . Oh, and take a flashlight, and don't forget to pack some spare batteries. . . . Why don't you take my jacket? It's a good idea to have something warm. . . . Now, you need to take a hat. You could borrow your dad's. But don't lose it. . . . Oh, and Jenny, do you want to pack some other shoes?

Jenny I'm sorry, Mom. Did you say something? I can't hear you with my headphones on.

> **Figure it out** →

B How many different ways can you make the suggestion *Take a flashlight*? Use the conversation above to help you.

3 Grammar *Advice and suggestions*

What **should** I take?	**Do you want to** pack some other shoes?
Should I take these shoes?	**Why don't you** take a hat?
You **should** take a hat.	**It's a good idea to** pack a jacket.
You **shouldn't** take high heels.	**Take** a flashlight.
You **could** borrow your dad's hat.	**Don't forget to** pack some batteries.
You **need to** have warm clothes.	

> **In conversation . . .**
>
> *You should* . . . can be very strong. People sometimes soften it by saying:
>
> *I think you should . . .*
> *Maybe you should (just) . . .*
> *You should probably . . .*

Complete the suggestions to someone going on these trips. Then compare with a partner.

1. backpacking in Australia

"I think you should _take a lot of sunscreen_ ."
"It's a good idea _____ ."
"Maybe you should _____ ."

3. a language course in Canada

"You need _____ ."
"It's a good idea _____ ."
"You could _____ ."

2. a trip to Paris

"Don't forget _____ ."
"Why don't you _____ ?"
"You could _____ ."

4. a hiking trip in the Andes

"You should probably _____ ."
"Maybe you shouldn't _____ ."
"Take _____ ."

4 Vocabulary notebook *Travel items*

See page 74 for a new way to log and learn vocabulary.

That's a great idea.

1 Conversation strategy *Responding to suggestions*

A Look at the responses to the suggestion. Who really wants to go hiking?

A We should go hiking together sometime.

☐ *B That sounds like fun.*   ☐ *C Well, I'd like to, but . . .*   ☐ *D I guess we could, maybe.*

Now listen. What would Chris like to do? What does Adam think?

Chris	You know, we should take a few days off sometime.
Adam	Yeah, we should. Definitely.
Chris	We could go to Mexico or something.
Adam	That's a great idea.
Chris	We could even go for a couple of weeks.
Adam	Well, maybe. I guess we could, but . . .
Chris	You know, we could just quit our jobs and maybe go backpacking for a few months. . . .
Adam	Well, I don't know. I'd like to, but . . . I guess I need to keep this job, you know, to pay for school and stuff.
Chris	Yeah, me too, I guess.

Notice how Adam responds to Chris's suggestions with expressions like these. Find examples in the conversation.

For suggestions you like:
That's a great idea.
That sounds great.
I'd love to.

For suggestions you don't like:
Maybe.
I guess we could, but . . .
I don't know.
I'd like to, but . . .

B Match the suggestions with the responses. Then practice with a partner.

1. You should come skiing with me sometime. __b__
2. Why don't we go somewhere on Sunday? _____
3. We could go camping together sometime. _____
4. Let's go traveling in Asia next year. _____
5. We should go to Paris to see the Louvre. _____
6. Why don't we go to Australia sometime? _____

a. That's a great idea. How's your French?
b. Oh, I'd love to. Are you a good skier?
c. I don't know. It's kind of far.
d. I'd like to, but I already have plans.
e. Maybe. I don't have a tent, though.
f. I guess we could. Where in Asia?

About you → **C** *Pair work* Practice again. Use your own responses, and continue each conversation.

SELF-STUDY
AUDIO CD
CD-ROM

2 Strategy plus I guess

You can use **I guess** when you're not 100% sure about something, or if you don't want to sound 100% sure.

I guess I need to keep this job.

Yeah, me too, I guess.

Listen. Check (✓) where you hear *I guess* in these conversations. Then practice with a partner.

In conversation . . .

I guess is one of the top 20 expressions.

1. *A* You know, ✓ my favorite kind of vacation is going camping.
   B Really? That sounds like fun ___ . We should do that sometime.
   A Yeah. ___ we could go next summer.

2. *A* ___ it gets pretty cold in Canada in the winter.
   B Oh, yeah. It's freezing cold sometimes. But ___ it's fun in the snow. You can ski and stuff.
   A Yeah, ___ I'd probably like the snow.

3. *A* I'm going to Lake Tahoe next weekend. Do you want to come?
   B Well, ___ I could go. Oh, wait, ___ I have an exam next week. But I could study in the car ___ .

4. *A* You know, ___ we don't get away very often.
   B Yeah. Two weeks' vacation a year isn't enough ___ .
   A But ___ we could go away on weekends or something.

3 Listening and speaking It's good to travel.

A Look at these sentences about travel. How would you complete them? Then listen to Michael and Diana. Are any of your ideas the same?

1. "Everyone should travel to _____ sometime."
2. "Everyone should learn _____ ."
3. "World cultures should be a required _____ in _____ ."
4. "It's a good idea to travel with _____ ."
5. "You should _____ about a place before you go there."
6. "It's nice to try _____ in a new country."

B *Group work* Discuss Michael's and Diana's statements. Do you agree with them? Say why or why not.

A I guess I agree with the first sentence. I mean, it's good to visit other countries.
B Definitely. But some people can't afford to travel.

4 Free talk Travel smart!

See *Free talk 7* at the back of the book for more speaking practice.

Interesting places

1 Reading

A Brainstorm! Do you ever stay in hotels? What's fun about staying in a hotel? Make a class list.

> You don't have to cook or make your bed.   You can sit by the pool to relax.

B Look at the article quickly. Where are these unusual hotels? Then read the article. Which hotel would you like to stay in? Why? Tell a partner.

Somewhere different...

Three of our fearless travel reporters checked out some very unusual hotels.

Dive into the lobby....

Most divers go underwater to see fish and coral reefs. But in Florida, in the U.S., you can also stay at the world's only underwater hotel. It takes about an hour to dive down to the **Jules Undersea Lodge**. Then you swim up into the pool in the lobby to check in. The rooms are small, so you should only take a few things. Fortunately, the hotel packs them in a waterproof container and takes them there for you.

Salt, salt, everywhere . . .

The **Hotel de la Playa** in Bolivia is certainly different. It's almost completely made of salt – the walls, tables, chairs, and even the beds. Everything except the toilets! While we were there, we visited Fisherman's Island with its fabulous 12-foot cacti. It's fun to rent mountain bikes to go and see the salt hills, lakes, and hot springs. Just be sure to take sunglasses – the sun gets extremely bright.

A place to chill out . . .

It's a pretty long way to go to stay at the **Ishotellet** (Ice Hotel) – 100 miles north of the Arctic Circle in Sweden. But it's definitely worth the effort. It's hard to imagine sleeping on an ice bed, but with a reindeer skin and a good sleeping bag, I was warm. And my wake-up call came with a hot drink. You can always go to the sauna to get warm, too. The hotel has an art gallery, a chapel, a movie theater, a disco, and a fabulous ice fireplace in the lounge. Make sure you check out of the hotel before it melts in the spring! But don't worry – they rebuild it every winter.

C Read the article again. Can you find this information?

1. How do you get to the Jules Undersea Lodge?
2. How long does it take to get to the Jules Undersea Lodge?
3. What are three interesting things to see near the Hotel de la Playa?
4. Why do you need sunglasses at the Hotel de la Playa?
5. What facilities do they have at the Ice Hotel?
6. Why do they have to rebuild the Ice Hotel every year?

2 Listening and writing Recommendations

A Look at these hotels. Which hotel would you like to visit? Why?

❶ The Cave Hotel

❷ The Lighthouse Hotel

❸ The Spa Hotel

B Read the advice about staying at these hotels. Can you match each piece of advice with a hotel? Then listen and check your guesses.

1. You should bring lots of books and board games for rainy days. _____
2. Wear flat shoes so you can climb the ladder to your room. _____
3. Be sure to take everything you need. It's miles from anywhere. _____
4. I really recommend the hot-air balloon ride. _____
5. Don't spend too much time in the water. _____
6. It's a good idea to have some binoculars to watch the dolphins. _____

C Imagine you are staying at one of the hotels in this lesson. Write a postcard to a classmate about your stay.

> **▶ Help note**
>
> **Writing postcards**
>
> | | |
> |---|---|
> | Start like this: → | Dear (name), / Hi there! |
> | Say if you are enjoying your stay: → | I'm having a great / fabulous / awful time here in . . . |
> | Describe the place, food, or weather: → | The food / weather / hotel is . . . |
> | Say something you did: → | It's a great place to . . . / Today I . . . |
> | Say something you are going to do: → | Tomorrow I'm going to . . . |
> | End like this: → | See you soon! / See you next week! / Love, |
> | | (your name) |

To: _____

_____

Vocabulary notebook

Travel items

Learning tip *Writing notes about nouns*

When you write down a new noun, it's a good idea to write notes about it.

its pronunciation and stress →	<u>phrase</u> book (ph = /f/)
if it's a countable or an uncountable noun →	sunscreen (uncountable)
	a map (countable)
the spelling of the singular and plural forms →	a hairbrush, hairbrush(es)
if it's always plural →	sunglasses (always plural)
how to make a plural noun singular →	a pair of sunglasses (singular)

1 Match the travel items to the notes. Mark the stress on each word by underlining the stressed syllable.

1. <u>bath</u>ing suit __d__
2. batteries _____
3. clothes _____
4. schedule _____
5. scissors _____

a. (*sc* = /s/), plural, *a pair of* (singular)
b. (sounds almost like *close*), always plural
c. (*sch* = /sk/), countable
d. (*ui* in *suit* sounds like *oo* in *too*), countable
e. *ies* = *y* (singular)

A pair of shoes

The top items people talk about with ***a pair of*** are:

1. shoes
2. pants
3. shorts
4. jeans
5. glasses
6. stockings
7. socks
8. gloves

2 Add two more travel items. Then write notes about each word.

Items	Notes
1. pajamas	
2. toothpaste	
3. shampoo	
4. razor	
5.	
6.	

On your own

Look through some travel brochures, and find two different types of vacations. List 10 items you need for each one.

At home

In Unit 8, you learn how to . . .

- use *Whose . . . ?* and *mine*, *yours*, *his*, *hers*, etc.
- order adjectives before nouns and the pronouns *one* and *ones*.
- talk about your home, your belongings, and your habits.
- use *Do you mind . . . ?* to ask for permission and
  Would you mind . . . ? to make requests.
- agree to requests in different ways.

in the closet

on a shelf

on the desk

in a box

1

on top of the dresser

in a drawer

3

under the bed

on the floor

4

Before you begin . . .

Look at the pictures. What do you keep in these places?
Are you a pack rat? Do you hate to throw things away?

John There's so much stuff in here! Are all these things really ours? I mean, whose bathing suit is this? Is it yours or your grandmother's?

Sandra Hey, it's mine, and I like it.

John And whose clothes are these?

Sandra Oh, they're my sister's. She's storing some things here while she's away. The jewelry's hers, too. Ugh, look at these awful earrings. She has such weird taste.

John But those are yours. I bought them for you!

Sandra Oh, you did? Sorry. I guess they're not so bad.

1 Getting started

A 🖸 Listen. John and Sandra are cleaning out their closet. What do they find? Practice the conversation.

> **Figure it out** → **B** Can you complete the sentences? Use the conversation above to help you. Then compare with a partner.

❶ *A* _____ stuff is this? ❷ *A* Is this bathing suit yours? ❸ *A* Are these your sister's earrings?

    B It's ours.   *B* Yes, it's _____ .   *B* Yes, they're _____ .

2 Grammar *Whose . . . ?; possessive pronouns* 💿

Whose bathing suit is this?	It's **my** bathing suit.	It's **mine**.
Whose jewelry is this?	They're **your** earrings.	They're **yours**.
Whose clothes are these?	It's **her** jewelry.	It's **hers**.
	They're **his** shoes.	They're **his**.
	They're **our** things.	They're **ours**.
	It's **their** stuff.	It's **theirs**.

> **In conversation . . .**
>
> 20% of the uses of *mine* are in the expression *friend(s) of mine*.

A Complete the conversations with possessive pronouns. Then ask and answer the questions with a partner. Give your own answers.

1. *A* Where do you keep your photos?
   B Well, I keep ____mine____ in a box under my bed.
   My sister keeps _____ in an album. My parents
   put _____ in frames on the wall, and my brother
   throws _____ on the floor!

2. *A* Do you ever lose your keys? I'm always losing _____ .
   B No. We always keep _____ on top of the refrigerator.

3. *A* What do you do with your old clothes?
   B Sometimes I give things to a friend of _____ .
   My sisters keep _____ for years. But my mom gives
   _____ to charity.

4. *A* How long do you keep your credit card receipts?
   B Just till the bill comes. How long do you keep _____ ?
   A I keep _____ for months.

About you → **B** *Group work* Put two of your belongings onto a group table. Take turns choosing items and asking who they belong to.

A **Whose wallet is this?**
B **I think it's Victor's.**
C **It's not mine. It's Luisa's.**

3 Speaking naturally *Grammatical words*

A **Where *do you* keep *your* CDs?**
B **On a shelf *next to* my CD player. Where *do you* keep yours?**
A **In a pile *on the* floor *by* my bed.**

A 💿 Listen and repeat the conversation above. Notice how grammatical words like *do, you, your, my, a, the, in, on, next to,* and *by* are reduced in these sentences.

About you → **B** *Pair work* Make conversations like the one above. Use the ideas below or add your own.

- CDs
- magazines
- DVDs
- passport / ID
- sports equipment

1 Building vocabulary

A 🎧 Listen and say the words. Check (✓) the things you like. Then tell a partner.

"I like the armchair. It looks really comfortable."

Bedroom

- ☐ clock
- ☐ curtains
- ☐ dresser
- ☐ nightstand
- ☐ carpet

Bathroom

- ☐ mirror
- ☐ shower
- ☐ toilet
- ☐ sink
- ☐ bathtub

Living room

- ☐ armchair
- ☐ lamp
- ☐ coffee table
- ☐ cushions
- ☐ end table
- ☐ sofa

Kitchen

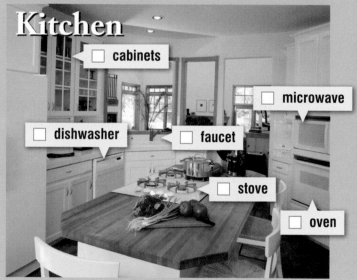

- ☐ cabinets
- ☐ microwave
- ☐ dishwasher
- ☐ faucet
- ☐ stove
- ☐ oven

Word sort → **B** Complete the chart with things in your home. Then compare with a partner.

Living room	Kitchen	My room	Other
sofa	microwave		

A In our living room, there's a sofa and . . .
B We don't have a sofa. We have a couple of armchairs and . . .

2 Building language

A 🔵 Listen to these people at a department store. Which items do they like?

Meg Hmm. The rug in the middle is nice, and I like that red one, too. Which one do you like?

Lia I like all of them. They're all nice.

Jon Those small round speakers are cool.

Andy Which ones? The little silver ones?

Jon Yeah. The ones on the right.

Figure it out

B *Pair work* Can you complete these conversations? Then practice with a partner.

1 *A* Which rug do you like? Do you like the blue _____ ?

   B Not really. I like the _____ one _____ .

2 *A* Which speakers do you like? The silver _____ ?

   B Um, no, I like the _____ ones.

3 Grammar *Order of adjectives; pronouns* one *and* ones 🔵

Usual adjective order:

opinion, size, color, shape, nationality, material

They have **beautiful Turkish** rugs.

I like the **big red** rug.

I want those **cute little round** speakers.

I like the green rug. Which **one** do you like?

   I like the blue **one** in the middle.

Those speakers are cool. Which **ones** do you like?

   I like the silver **ones** on the right.

▶ **In conversation . . .**

People usually use just one or two adjectives before a noun.

Complete the statements and questions about these things. Then compare with a partner.

I like the _____ .

Which _____ do you like?

I don't like the _____ .

Which _____ do you like?

I'd like to buy the _____ .

Which _____ would you like?

4 Vocabulary notebook *The ABCs of home*

See page 84 for a new way to log and learn vocabulary.

Do you mind . . . ?

1 Conversation strategy *Asking politely*

A In which request is someone (a) asking you to do something? (b) asking permission to do something?

Would you mind opening the window? _____
Do you mind if I open the window? _____

 **Now listen. What does Ben ask Jessica?**

Ben	Hello! Come on in.
Jessica	These are for you, Ben. Are the others here yet?
Ben	Oh, thank you. No, not yet. So just make yourself at home. Can I take your coat?
Jessica	Sure. Thanks. This is a great apartment! Do you mind if I look around?
Ben	No, go ahead.
Jessica	Oh, I love this antique table.
Ben	Yeah, it's great, but it's not really mine. It's my mother's.
Jessica	It's beautiful.
Ben	Yeah, thanks. Listen, I hate to ask this, but would you mind helping me in the kitchen? I'm running a bit late.
Jessica	No, not at all. What can I do?
Ben	Well, . . . could you chop the onions?
Jessica	No problem. I'm happy to help.

Notice how Jessica uses *Do you mind . . . ?* to ask for permission, and Ben uses *Would you mind . . . ?* to ask Jessica to do something. Also notice that they answer no to show they agree. Find the examples in the conversation.

> "Do you mind . . . ?"
>   "No, go ahead."
>
> "Would you mind . . . ?"
>   "No, not at all."

B *Pair work* Student A: Imagine you are visiting your partner's home. Ask permission to do these things. Student B: Agree to your partner's requests. Then change roles.

1. _____ use your phone?
2. _____ put on a CD?
3. _____ open a window?
4. _____ take a cookie?
5. _____ get a glass of water
6. _____ turn on the TV?

"Do you mind if I use your phone?"   *"No, go ahead."*

C *Pair work* Student A: Imagine your partner is visiting your home. Ask him or her to do these things. Student B: Agree to your partner's requests. Then change roles.

1. answer the door for me
2. hand me the newspaper
3. set the table for me
4. make some coffee
5. help me with the dishes
6. feed the cat

"Would you mind answering the door for me?"   *"No, not at all."*

SELF-STUDY
AUDIO CD
CD-ROM

2 Strategy plus *Agreeing to requests*

Answer *Yes* to agree to requests with *Can* and *Could*:	Answer *No* to agree to requests with *mind*:

Can I use your phone?
    Yes. / Sure. / Go (right) ahead.
	Do you mind if I use your phone?
	    No, go (right) ahead. / No, not at all.

Could you chop the onions?
    Yes. / Sure. / OK. / No problem.
	Would you mind helping me in the kitchen?
	    No, not at all. / Oh, no. No problem.

▶ *In conversation . . .*

Do you mind _____*ing?* and
Would you mind if I . . . ?
are possible but not very common.

Complete the answers. Then practice with a partner.

1. *A* I hate to ask this, but would you mind turning off your cell phone during dinner?

   B _____ . But do you mind if I make just one quick call?

2. *A* Do you mind if I use your computer to check my e-mail?

   B _____ . Go right ahead.

3. *A* Can I borrow your cell phone for a few minutes?

   B Well, I'm expecting a call, but _____ .

4. *A* Would you mind helping me with dinner tonight?

   B _____ . What are you making?

5. *A* Could you get some milk when you go to the supermarket?

   B _____ . What kind do you want?

3 Listening *Could I ask a favor?*

A Listen to these conversations between roommates. Can you guess each request? Complete the sentences.

	Agrees	Doesn't agree
1. Can you get me a _____ ?	☐	☐
2. Do you mind if I borrow some _____ ?	☐	☐
3. Would you mind getting me the _____ ?	☐	☐
4. Do you mind if I borrow one of your _____ ?	☐	☐

B Now listen to the complete conversations. Check your answers, and listen to find out if each person agrees to the request. Check (✓) the boxes.

4 Free talk *All about home*

See *Free talk 8* at the back of the book for more speaking practice.

Home habits

1 Reading

A Discuss these statements with a partner. How many are true for you?

- I make my bed every morning.
- I do the dishes right after I eat.
- I organize my books and CDs.
- I always turn off the light when I leave a room.
- I keep my magazines for about six months.
- I use a dozen different cleaning products.

B Read the article. How do your home habits compare with the ones in the article?

AT HOME – How **typical** are you?

Do you make your bed every day? Do you try to save electricity at home? Are you a pack rat? Read about the home habits of Americans – are they the same as yours?

Making beds and doing dishes

74% of people make their beds every morning. 5% *never* do. And 3% actually change their sheets every day.

Do you wash the dishes right after eating? 58% of Americans do, but 5% let theirs sit for two or more days!

Neat and tidy

Are you an organized person? 13% of people alphabetize their books and CDs, or organize them in some way!

The average home has 13 cleaning products around the house.

Pack rats

How long do you save magazines? About half the population throws away old ones after six months. But 20% keep them for years and years.

Lights out

Are you careful about saving electricity? 25% of people turn off the light when they leave a room. 8% never do. Four out of five leave the lights on when they go out at night.

Who does the laundry?

Men do 29% of the 419 million loads of laundry washed each week. Almost all unmarried men do at least one load a week.

C Fill in the missing information from the article. Then discuss with a partner. Which facts do you find interesting? Which are surprising?

1. 74% of people in the U.S. __make their beds__ every morning.
2. 58% of them _____ right after eating.
3. _____ of Americans never turn off the light when they leave a room.
4. _____ of them organize their books and CDs.
5. 50% of all Americans _____ after six months.
6. Almost all umarried men in the U.S. _____ .

A Most people make their beds. I think that's surprising. I don't make mine every day.
B No, me neither. I don't have time. I also think it's interesting that . . .

2 Listening and writing *Evening routines*

A Do you do any of these things when you get home every day? Tell the class.

B Listen. What does Mario do when he gets home? Number the pictures above in the order he does things. Is your evening like Mario's?

C *Group survey* Take turns answering the questions. Take notes on your classmates' answers.

- What do you do as soon as you get home?
- Do you change your clothes first? What do you do next?
- What do you do before you have dinner?

- Do you watch TV while you're eating?
- Do you do the dishes right after dinner?
- Do you have a snack before you go to bed?
- What's your bedtime routine?

A OK, so what do you do as soon as you get home? I check my phone messages.
B Really? I always get a glass of water or something.

D Use your notes to write a short article about the evening routines in your group. Use the headings below.

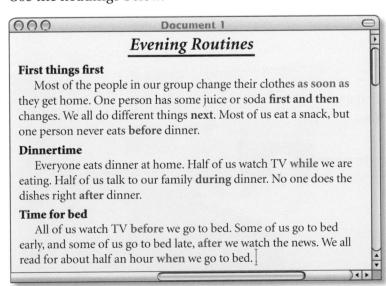

Document 1

Evening Routines

First things first

Most of the people in our group change their clothes **as soon as** they get home. One person has some juice or soda **first and then** changes. We all do different things **next**. Most of us eat a snack, but one person never eats **before** dinner.

Dinnertime

Everyone eats dinner at home. Half of us watch TV **while** we are eating. Half of us talk to our family **during** dinner. No one does the dishes right **after** dinner.

Time for bed

All of us watch TV **before** we go to bed. Some of us go to bed early, and some of us go to bed late, **after** we watch the news. We all read for about half an hour **when** we go to bed.

> **Help note**

Ordering events

- To show a sequence:
  first, next, (and) then

- Before a noun:
  before / after
  during = "at the same time as"

- To link actions:
  when
  as soon as = "immediately after," "right after"
  while = "at the same time as"
  before / after

Learning tip *Alphabet game*

Make learning new words into a game! Choose a topic
and try to think of a word for each letter of the alphabet.

1 Label the pictures. The first letter of each word is given for you.

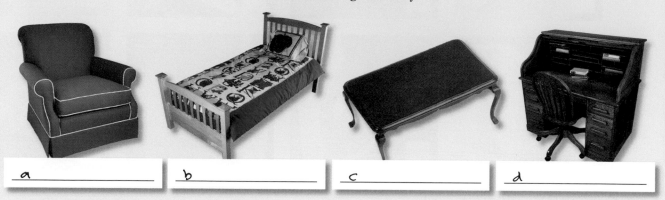

a _____   b _____   c _____   d _____

2 Now complete your own alphabet chart. Can you think of something in your home
for each letter?

a	armchair	j		s	
b		k		t	
c		l		u	
d		m		v	
e		n		w	
f		o		x	
g		p		y	
h		q		z	
i		r			

On your own

Make labels for different things in your home.
Don't throw the label away until you can
remember the new word.

Things happen

In Unit 9, you learn how to . . .

- use the past continuous for events in progress in the past.
- use *myself*, *yourself*, *himself*, etc.
- talk about accidents and things that went wrong.
- react to other people's stories.
- use the expression *I bet* . . . .

Before you begin . . .

Look at the pictures. Think about a time one of these things happened to you. Tell the class about a time when you . . .

- broke something.
- forgot something.
- lost something.
- damaged something.

When things go wrong . . .

Are you having a bad week?

Sean Davis

" Actually, yes. I was going to work on the train Monday morning, and I was talking to this woman. I guess I wasn't paying attention, and I missed my stop. I was half an hour late for a meeting with my new boss. "

Julia Chen

" Oh, definitely! A friend of mine accidentally deleted all my music files yesterday when she was using my computer. I tried for hours to find them, but nothing worked. I lost everything! "

Roberto Moreno

" Yeah, kind of. A couple of days ago, a friend and I were trying to look cool in front of some girls at the mall. We weren't looking, and we walked right into a glass door. I was so embarrassed. "

1 Getting started

A 🔘 Listen and read. Why is each person having a bad week?

Figure it out **B** Can you choose the correct verb forms in these sentences? Use the information above to help you. Then compare with a partner.

1. Sean **talked / was talking** to a woman on the train, and he **missed / was missing** his stop.
2. Julia's friend **deleted / was deleting** her files when she **used / was using** Julia's computer.
3. Roberto and his friend **tried / were trying** to look cool when they **walked / were walking** into a glass door.

2 Grammar Past continuous statements 💿

> **Use the past continuous to set the background for a story or tell about events in progress in the past. Use the simple past for completed actions in the past.**
>
> I **was talking** to a woman, and I **missed** my stop. I **wasn't paying** attention.
> We **were trying** to look cool, and we **walked** into a glass door. We **weren't looking**.
>
> A friend of mine deleted all my files **when** she was using my computer.
> **When** my friend was using my computer, she deleted all my files.

> **▶ In conversation . . .**
>
> The most common verbs in the past continuous are *talk*, *do*, *go*, *say*, *try*, *get*, and *tell*.

A Complete the anecdotes with the past continuous or simple past.

1. A few weeks ago, when I __was making__ (make) dinner, my friend
   _____ (call). I completely _____ (forget) about the
   food on the stove, and I _____ (burn) everything!

2. I _____ (damage) my parents' car last week. I _____
   (drive) to work, and I _____ (run) into a stop sign. Now I have
   to pay for the repairs.

3. Last week, I _____ (hurt) my foot when I _____ (do)
   aerobics. I don't know why, but I just _____ (fall). I felt so stupid.

4. I _____ (have) lunch in a restaurant yesterday when the server
   accidentally _____ (spill) water all over me! It was embarrassing,
   but then I _____ (get) my lunch for free.

5. My friend and I _____ (talk) in class, and we _____
   (not pay) attention. Suddenly we realized the teacher _____
   (stand) right beside us. He and the whole class _____ (listen) to us!

B *Pair work* Choose one of the anecdotes above, and retell it to a partner.
Try not to look at the text.

3 Speaking naturally Fall-rise intonation

> I was running for a bus last week, and I fell.
>
> When I was going home yesterday, I ran into an old friend.

A 💿 Listen and repeat the sentences above. Notice that the intonation falls and then
rises slightly at the end of the first part of each sentence. This sets the background.

> **About**
> **you**

B Think of a short anecdote about something that happened to you this week.
Take turns telling a partner.

1 Building vocabulary

A Listen and say the words and sentences. How many of these words and expressions do you already know?

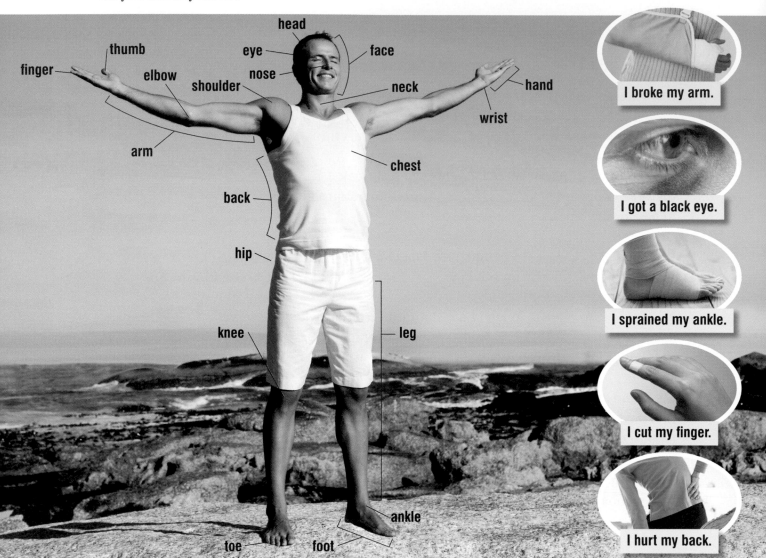

head

eye   face

nose   neck

thumb

finger   elbow

shoulder   wrist

arm   hand

back   chest

hip

knee   leg

toe   foot   ankle

I broke my arm.

I got a black eye.

I sprained my ankle.

I cut my finger.

I hurt my back.

Word sort → **B** Make true sentences about accidents that happened to you or people you know. Complete the chart.

break	sprain	cut	hurt
I broke my leg.		My dad cut his hand.	

About you → **C** *Pair work* Take turns telling about the accidents in your chart.

"I broke my leg when I was ten. I fell when I was riding my bike."

2 Building language

A Listen. What happened to Barry? What was he doing? Practice the conversation.

Nicole So how was your ski trip? Did you have a good time?
Barry Yeah, I guess. I sort of had an accident.
Nicole Oh, really? What happened? Did you hurt yourself?
Barry Yeah, I broke my leg.
Nicole Oh, no! How did it happen? I mean, what were you doing?
Barry Well, actually, I was talking on my cell phone. . . .
Nicole While you were skiing? That's kind of dangerous.
Barry Yeah, I know. But I was by myself, so I was lucky I had my cell to call for help.

Figure it out → **B** Find the questions in the conversation. Which are past continuous, and which are simple past?

3 Grammar *Past continuous questions; reflexive pronouns*

Past continuous	**Simple past**		
Were you **skiing** with a friend?	**Did** you **hurt** yourself?	I	myself.
No, I wasn't. I was by myself.	Yes, I **did**.	You	yourself.
What were you **doing** (when you fell)?	**What did** you **do**?	He — hurt —	himself.
I was talking on my cell phone.	I **called** for help.	She	herself.
		We	ourselves.
		They	themselves.

A Match the sentences and follow-up questions. Then compare with a partner.

1. I burned myself last night. __c__
2. Did you notice my black eye? _____
3. My dad hurt himself at the gym. _____
4. I fell out of bed last night. _____
5. My sister sprained both her wrists. _____
6. My mom and I had a car accident. _____

a. Oh, no! Who was driving?
b. Did you hurt yourself?
c. Oh, were you cooking?
d. Yeah. How did you get it?
e. He did? What happened? Was he lifting weights?
f. How did that happen? What was she doing?

> **In conversation . . .**
>
> 10% of uses of *yourself* are in the question *How about yourself?* Almost 10% of uses of *myself* are in the expression *by myself*.

B *Pair work* Role-play conversations about the situations above. How long can you continue each conversation?

A **I burned myself last night.**
B **Oh, were you cooking?**
A **No, I was making some tea, and I . . .**

4 Vocabulary notebook *From head to toe*

See page 94 for a useful way to log and learn vocabulary.

That's really funny!

1 Conversation strategy *Reacting to a story*

A Can you choose the best responses to this anecdote? Check (✓) the boxes.

A *One time I arrived an hour early for dinner at my boss's house – I got the time wrong. And he was taking a shower!*

B ☐ Oh, that's funny.
☐ Yeah? Good.
☐ How embarrassing!
☐ That sounds nice.

Now listen. What happened to Matt?

Matt I was making Mexican food for a bunch of people one time. . . .

Emily Oh, I love Mexican.

Matt Anyway, everything was ready, and I picked up this big pot of rice, and I burned myself, and I dropped it right in the middle of the floor upside down!

Emily Oh, no.

Matt I freaked!

Emily Oh, I bet.

Matt So anyway, I just ran out to the restaurant down the street, bought some rice, put it in a bowl, and served dinner.

Emily I bet no one even noticed.

Matt They didn't. I was only gone for five minutes.

Emily That's really funny.

Notice how Emily reacts to Matt's story. She comments on the things he says to show she is interested and listening. Find examples in the conversation.

"I was making Mexican food . . ."
"Oh, I love Mexican."

B Read the story below and the comments on the right. For each part of the story, choose a comment. Practice telling the story and commenting with a partner.

1. I was working as a server at Pierre's last year. __c__
2. Yeah, it's a fancy place with sofas and everything. _____
3. Well, it's not cheap. Anyway, I was serving coffee to this guy one day, and I spilled it all over his suit! _____
4. Yeah – but wait. Then I found out the guy was Pierre! _____
5. Yeah, and he was pretty mad. But he didn't fire me! _____

a. Oh, no. I bet he was upset.
b. That was lucky.
c. Oh, I hear it's a nice place.
d. It sounds expensive.
e. You're kidding! The owner?

SELF-STUDY
AUDIO CD
CD-ROM

2 *Strategy plus* *I bet . . .*

You can start a statement with *I bet . . .* when you are pretty sure about something.

. . . and I served dinner.

I bet no one even noticed.

You can also use *I bet* as a response to show you understand a situation.

Matt I freaked!
Emily I bet.

▶ **In conversation . . .**

Bet is one of the top 600 words. Over 60% of its uses are in the expression **I bet . . . .**

A Choose a response from the box for each story below. Can you think of other responses? Then compare with a partner.

> I bet you were surprised.   I bet she was really embarrassed.
> I bet your parents weren't too happy.

1 *A* A friend of mine was staying at a hotel one time, and she was walking back to her room in the dark, and she fell in the pool!

   B _____ .

2 *A* I got on a plane one time and fell asleep right away. And when I woke up, I realized I was on the wrong flight.

   B Oh, _____ .

3 *A* I was on a trip with my parents a few years ago, and we were flying home. Anyway, we got to the airport, and I realized my passport was still at the hotel.

   B Oh, no. _____ .

B *Pair work* Choose one of the stories above, and add details to continue it. Then work with a partner. Take turns telling your stories and responding with *I bet . . . .*

3 *Listening* *Funny stories*

A 💿 Listen to the stories. Which comment goes with which story? Number the comments.

☐ *Oh, no! That's terrible.*   ☐ *I bet. That's amazing.*   ☐ *Oh! That's funny.*   ☐ *Oh, I bet that was boring.*

B 💿 Listen again. Think of a different comment for each story.

1. _____   3. _____

2. _____   4. _____

91

Good things happen.

1 Reading

A Brainstorm! Make a list of all the good things that happened to you recently. Tell the class.

> I found $20.   An old friend called me.   I passed my driver's test.

B Read the newspaper column. What good things happened to these people?

Around Town by Nelson Hunter

Acts of Kindness

A few weeks ago, I was walking to my car in the parking lot, when someone came up to me and said he enjoyed reading my weekly column. "But," he said, "you always write about everyone's bad experiences. Why don't you ask people to talk about their good experiences, too?"

So I asked readers to write in and tell me about all the good things that happened to them recently. I got hundreds of replies. Here are three of them:

I was coming home from a party really late at night, and I missed the last train home. I didn't have enough money for a cab, and I didn't want to walk home in the dark. I was standing outside the train station, and I guess I looked worried because a woman came up and asked me if I needed any help. She offered to share a cab with me and to pay for it! She said she didn't like being by herself at night, either. I was so grateful.

– Abby Walters

When I was shopping at the mall last week, I lost my wallet with all my money and credit cards in it. I spent a long time looking for it with no luck. I was really upset because it had my spare house key and my address in it, too. Anyway, later that day after I got home, my doorbell rang. It was a young man, and he had my wallet. Apparently, he saw it on the ground when he was walking into the mall. He drove all the way to my house to give it to me! I couldn't believe it! I was so lucky!   **– Andrea Keane**

After class each week, I often go to the local donut shop and get some coffee before I go home. When I was leaving the store last week, the owner gave me a bag of donuts from the day before to take home for free. She said I was a good customer, and she didn't want to throw them out. When I got home, I shared them with my roommates!   **– John Jones**

So, thank you for all the letters. For next week, I want to hear about any funny stories you have. What funny things happened to you recently?

C Read the article again. Are the sentences true or false? Correct the false sentences.

	True	False
1. Nelson Hunter usually writes about ~~good~~ *bad* things that happen to people.	☐	☑
2. Abby Walters had to pay for a cab home when she missed her train.	☐	☐
3. Andrea was worried because if someone found her wallet, they could get into her house.	☐	☐
4. A young man found Andrea's wallet when he was leaving the mall.	☐	☐
5. John ate the bag of donuts by himself.	☐	☐

2 Listening and speaking Happy endings

A  Listen to two stories. Answer the questions.

Gary's story
1. Where was Gary? What was he doing?
2. Who did he meet?
3. Why did he forget his briefcase?
4. What did he do when he got to work?
5. Does this story have a happy ending? Why? Why not?

Pam's story
1. Where was Pam going?
2. What was her problem?
3. How did she get help?
4. How did the woman offer to help?
5. Does this story have a happy ending? Why? Why not?

B *Pair work* Student A: Choose one of the stories above, and retell it to a partner.
Student B: Listen. Did your partner leave out any important details?

3 Writing Anecdotes

A Think of a good thing that happened to you recently. Write 10 to 12 sentences about it. Make sure your sentences are in order.

I was walking to work last week.	The light changed.
It started to rain.	I had to wait for a really long time.
I didn't have an umbrella.	A young man came up to me.
I put a newspaper over my head and ran.	He offered to share his umbrella.
I got to the corner.	He walked with me all the way to work!

B Now use your notes to write a letter to Nelson Hunter's column.

Dear Nelson,

   Last week, I was walking to work **when** it started to rain. I didn't have an umbrella, so I put a newspaper over my head and ran.

   When I got to the corner, the light changed, and I had to wait for a really long time. **While** I was waiting, a young man came up to me and offered to share his umbrella. He walked with me all the way to work! It was so nice of him.

Help note

Linking ideas with *when* and *while*

- You can use *when* or *while* to link a longer "background" event and another action.
- *While* emphasizes the length of time an action or event takes.
- *When* also shows events that happen one after another.

C *Class activity* Read your classmates' letters. Tell the class about one you read.

4 Free talk What was happening?

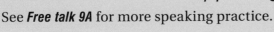

See *Free talk 9A* for more speaking practice.

Learning tip *Sketches*

Draw and label pictures to help you remember new vocabulary.

1 Label the sketch. Use the words in the box.

eye
nose
head
face
neck
shoulder

Take my hand . . .

The top 10 body parts
people talk about are:

1. hand	6. arm
2. eye	7. mouth
3. head	8. ear
4. face	9. back
5. leg	10. knee

2 Now make a sketch of a body from head to toe.
How many parts of the body can you label?

On your own

Before you go to sleep each night, think of the name for each part of your body. Start at your head, and work towards your toes. Can you think of each word in English before you fall asleep?

1 Can you complete this conversation?

A Complete the conversation. Use the simple past or past continuous of the verbs.

Marty How ___did___ you ___get___ (get) that black eye?
_____ you _____ (fall) or something?

Kevin Not exactly. I _____ (crash) into a tree.

Marty You're kidding! How _____ that _____ (happen)?

Kevin Well, I _____ (ride) my little brother's bicycle. And his friends _____ (watch) me and _____ (laugh) at me.

Marty Why _____ they _____ (laugh)? What _____ you _____ (do)?

Kevin I _____ (not do) anything. But the bike is kind of small.

Marty And I bet you _____ (try) to look cool, too.

Kevin I guess. I _____ (look) at the kids behind me. And I _____ (not see) the tree ahead of me. When my brother _____ (shout), "Watch out," I _____ (turn) around, but it was too late.

Marty Oh, no! _____ you _____ (hurt) yourself?

Kevin Well, I _____ (not break) anything. I just _____ (feel) stupid.

B *Pair work* Practice the conversation. Then practice again and change Marty's responses.

2 What's in the bathroom?

A Look at the picture for ten seconds, and try to remember where things are. Then close your book. How many sentences can you write?

1. A toothbrush is on the sink.

B *Pair work* Choose six items from the picture. Give your partner clues to guess the items. Then change roles.

A **You use it to clean your teeth.**
B **A toothbrush or toothpaste.**

3 Can you use these expressions?

Use these words and expressions to complete the conversation. Use capital letters where necessary.

whose	yours	one	red	would you mind	I bet	by myself	no, not at all
mine	hers	it was	bright	✓do you mind if	I guess	yourself	

Karen <u>Do you mind if</u> I come in? You look busy.

Trish No, make _____ at home. _____ handing me that paintbrush? The red _____ .

Karen _____ .

Trish Thanks. So, what do you think?

Karen Um, nice. I love the _____ _____ wall. Did you and your roommate do this together?

Trish No, actually, I did it all _____ . Nadia's away this week.

Karen Oh, is she? _____ this was a lot of work.

Trish Actually, no. _____ very easy to do.

Karen _____ room is this? Is it _____ or Nadia's?

Trish This one is _____ , and _____ is on the right.

Karen Um, does Nadia like these colors?

Trish I don't know. But I do! _____ I have an eye for color.

4 Suggestions, please!

Pair work Think of solutions to these problems. Then take turns making suggestions.

"I always get a bad sunburn in the summer."
"My bedroom is always a mess."
"I'm going camping in June, but I don't have any equipment."
"Ouch! I think I just sprained my wrist."

A ***I always get a bad sunburn in the summer.***
B ***Why don't you . . . ?***

5 Do you mind . . . ?

Role play Imagine you and your partner are in a car on a road trip. One of you is the driver. Take turns asking permission and making requests. Use the ideas below, and add your own.

- drive
- listen to the radio
- listen to a CD
- slow down
- open the window
- stop for a snack
- look at the map
- borrow some sunscreen
- eat one of your cookies

A ***Would you mind slowing down?***
B ***No, not at all.***

Self-check

How sure are you about these areas
Circle the percentages.

grammar
20% 40% 60% 80% 100%
vocabulary
20% 40% 60% 80% 100%
conversation strategies
20% 40% 60% 80% 100%

. . . .

Study plan

What do you want to review?
Circle the lessons.
grammar
7A 7B 8A 8B 9A 9B
vocabulary
7A 7B 8A 8B 9A 9B
conversation strategies
7C 8C 9C

Communication

In Unit 10, you learn how to . . .

- make comparisons with adjectives.
- use *more* and *less* with nouns and verbs.
- talk about different ways of communicating.
- manage phone conversations.
- interrupt and restart conversations on the phone.
- use *just* to soften things you say.

2

With _____, you can have a business meeting with people in different places.

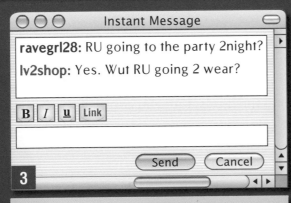

1

With _____, you and a friend can use your computers like phones, but you can also see each other.

4

Message:
Are we still on
for tomorrow?

OK   ABC

With _____, you can send written messages on your cell phone.

Instant Message

ravegrl28: RU going to the party 2night?

lv2shop: Yes. Wut RU going 2 wear?

B *I* u Link

Send   Cancel

3

With _____, you can have a written conversation online. You can write something to a friend and get a response instantly.

Before you begin . . .

Complete the sentences with the words below.
Do you use any of these ways of communicating?

- text messaging
- a webcam
- video conferencing
- instant messaging

Keeping in touch

How do you keep in touch with people?

Alma Jones

"I usually use e-mail. It's quicker and easier than anything else. But I get a lot of spam. There's nothing worse than spam when you're really busy."

Tim Henry

"I like to write letters. I know regular mail is slower than e-mail, but letters are more personal. And I never send those e-cards. I just think it's nicer to get a real card."

Mayumi Sat

"I send text messages to my friends all day. It's more fun than calling. And you can send photos, too. Too bad I can't do it in class."

Kayla Johnson

"Well, at work we use video conferencing. It's less expensive than a business trip. And more convenient. And you don't get jet lag, either!"

Paco Rodriguez

"I use a webcam to keep in touch with my parents. They think it's better than the phone because they can see me. I guess it's more interesting."

1 Getting started

A 🔘 Listen to the responses to the survey. How do these people keep in touch?

Figure it out

B Are these sentences true or false? Check (✓) the boxes. Can you correct the false ones? Then compare with a partner.

	True	False
1. Alma says e-mail is slower than anything else.	☐	☐
2. Tim thinks real cards are nicer than e-cards.	☐	☐
3. Mayumi thinks text messages are less fun than phone calls.	☐	☐
4. Kayla says video conferences are more expensive than business trips.	☐	☐
5. Paco's parents think webcam calls are better than phone calls.	☐	☐

2 Grammar *Comparative adjectives*

		Notice:
Adjective + -er (short adjectives)	E-mail is quick**er** than regular mail. It's easi**er**, too. It's nic**er** to get a real card than an e-card.	slow → slow**er** nice → nic**er**
more + adjective **less + adjective**	Letters are **more** personal than e-mail. Video conferences are **less** expensive than trips.	easy → eas**ier** big → big**ger**
good → better **bad → worse**	Webcams are **better** than regular phone calls. Spam is **worse** than regular junk mail.	**But:** fun → **more** fun

A Complete these sentences with the comparative form of the adjectives (↑ = more; ↓ = less).

1. E-mail is ___cheaper___ (↑ cheap) than regular mail.
2. E-cards are _____ (↑ hard) to open than real cards.
3. It's _____ (↓ convenient) to send a letter than an e-mail.
4. E-mail is good, but instant messaging is _____ (↑ good).
5. Webcam calls are _____ (↑ nice) than phone calls.
6. Text messages are _____ (↑ fun) than phone calls.
7. It's terrible to lose your cell phone, but it's _____ (↑ bad) to lose your laptop.
8. Cell-phone calls are _____ (↓ expensive) than regular phone calls.

> **In conversation . . .**
>
> The top adjectives after **more** are **expensive**, **convenient**, **important**, **interesting**, and **fun**.

About you → **B** **Group work** Do you agree with the sentences above? Discuss your ideas.

A *I agree that e-mail is cheaper than regular mail.*
B *Well, I don't know. Internet service is more expensive than stamps.*
C *Well, it depends. If you send a lot of mail, then Internet service is cheaper.*

3 Speaking naturally *Linking*

With e-mail, it's easier to keep in touch with people.

Text messages are less expensive than phone calls.

It's nicer to get a real card than an e-card.

A Listen and repeat the sentences above. Notice how the marked words are linked.

About you → **B** Now listen and repeat these questions. Then discuss the questions in groups.

1. Are you good at keeping in touch with people?
2. How do you keep in touch with friends and family?
3. Do you use a cell phone every day?
4. Do you ever send or get e-cards?
5. How often do you get instant messages or text messages?

1 Building vocabulary

A 🖳 Listen and read. What problems does John have getting through to Sandra?

1

Receptionist Sun Company.
John Could I speak to Sandra Bell, please?
Receptionist One moment, please.

5

Sandra Hello?
John Hi, Sandra. Guess what!
Sandra Hello? John? I can't hear you. We have a bad connection. Call me back on my office phone.

2

Voice mail Sandra Bell is on the phone. Please leave a message.
John Hi, Sandra. This is John. Call me back at the office.

3

Sandra Sandra Bell.
John Hi, Sandra. It's John. Did you get my message?
Sandra Uh, yes, I think so. Oh, hold on. I have another call. Call me later, OK?

4

Man Village Bakery.
John Oh, I'm sorry. I think I have the wrong number.
Man No problem.

6

Sandra Sandra Bell.
John Sandra! Listen. My boss has two tickets to . . . Oooh! We got cut off.

Word sort → **B** Find these expressions in the phone conversations, and write them in the chart. Then practice the conversations with a partner.

What can you say when you . . .	
hear a lot of noise on the line?	
start a voice-mail message?	
ask to speak to someone?	
call a stranger by mistake?	
want someone to return your call?	

2 Building language

A Listen to the conversation John and Sandra finally have. Why was John calling?

John Finally! It's hard to get ahold of you.

Sandra You're not that easy to reach, either.

John You spend a lot more time on the phone than I do.

Sandra That's because I get more calls.

John You just talk more! Anyway, I was calling before 'cause my boss had free tickets to the Sting concert tonight.

Sandra Oh, great! What time?

John Well, it's too late now. He gave them to someone else.

Sandra Oh, no! Why didn't you send me a text message?

Figure it out

B Now look at these sentences. Can you find sentences in the conversation with a similar meaning?

1.   John I spend less time on the phone than you.
2. Sandra You get fewer calls than I do.
3.   John I talk less than you do.

3 Grammar *More, less, fewer*

With countable nouns	**With uncountable nouns**	**With verbs**
I get **more** calls than you (do).	I spend **more** time on the phone.	She talks **more** than he does.
You get **fewer** calls than I do.	You spend **less** time on the phone.	He talks **less** than she does.

About you

A What's your style of communication? Make true sentences with *more*, *less*, or *fewer.*

1. I use a regular phone _____ than a cell phone.
2. I spend _____ time on the phone than my parents do.
3. When I'm on the phone, I talk _____ than I listen.
4. I make _____ calls during the day than at night.
5. I get _____ phone messages than e-mails.
6. I do _____ text messaging than instant messaging.
7. I write _____ letters than I did two years ago.

> **In conversation . . .**
>
> **Fewer** is not very common. People use it more in writing.

B *Group work* Discuss the sentences above. Compare your styles of communication.

A *I use a regular phone less than a cell phone.*

B *Oh, me too. I always have my cell phone with me, and . . .*

What were you saying?

1 Conversation strategy *Dealing with interruptions*

A How do you interrupt a conversation politely in your language? Do you use expressions like these?

> **A** *Hi, how are you?*
>
> **B** *Good. Oh, just a minute – someone's at the door! Can you hold on?*

Now listen. What does Maria want to tell Lucy?

Lucy	**Hello?**
Maria	**Hi, Lucy. It's Maria.**
Lucy	**Hey. How are you doing?**
Maria	**Great! Guess what? You remember that photo contest I entered?**
Lucy	**Yeah? Oh, just a minute. There's someone at the door. . . . So, you were saying?**
Maria	**Well, I won a trip to Mexico. . . .**
Lucy	**No way! Oh, sorry. Hold on a second. I just need to switch phones. . . . So, what were you saying?**
Maria	**Well, it's a trip for two, and I was just calling to ask . . . do you want to come with me?**
Lucy	**Are you kidding? Of course!**

Notice how Lucy interrupts the conversation and comes back to it with expressions like these. Find examples in the conversation.

Interrupting a conversation:	Restarting the conversation:
Just a minute / second.	*What were you saying?*
Excuse me just a second.	*You were saying?*
I'm sorry. Hold on (a second).	*Where were we?*
Could / Can you hold on a second?	*What were we talking about?*

B *Pair work* Student A: Think of some good news. Then "call" and tell your partner the news. Student B: "Answer" your partner's call. Interrupt and restart the conversation twice, using the ideas below. Then change roles.

- your dinner is burning
- the bathtub is overflowing
- you just spilled your coffee
- your cell phone is ringing

SELF-STUDY AUDIO CD CD-ROM

2 Strategy plus *just*

You can use the word *just* to make the things you say softer.

Just a minute.

I just need to switch phones.

I was just calling to ask . . .

▶ **In conversation . . .**

Just is one of the top 30 words.

Find two places to add *just* to each of these phone conversations. Then practice with a partner.

1. *A* Hello.
   B Hi, Dad. It's me. Is Mom there?
   A Yeah. But hold on a second. She's upstairs. I need to call her.

2. *A* Do you have a minute? I want to tell you some interesting news.
   B One second. I want to close the door. OK, so what were you saying?

3. *A* Is this a good time to talk?
   B Sure. I need to turn down the TV. What's up?
   A I was calling to ask about your new job. How do you like it?

4. *A* Hi. How are you? I'm calling to say hello.
   B Oh, hi. Listen, can I call you back? I have to finish something.

3 Listening *Sorry about that!*

A Listen to these phone conversations. Why is each person calling? Write the reasons below the pictures.

❶

❷

❸

B Listen again. Check (✓) the reason for the interruption in each conversation.

1. ☐ *It started to rain.*
   ☐ *He got another call.*
   ☐ *It was his turn to play golf.*

2. ☐ *He needed to find his wallet.*
   ☐ *Someone waved at him.*
   ☐ *He wanted to drink his soda.*

3. ☐ *There was a bad connection.*
   ☐ *The game started.*
   ☐ *The pizza arrived.*

4 Vocabulary notebook *Phone talk*

See page 106 for a new way to log and learn vocabulary.

1 Reading

A Can you match these text messages with their meanings? Compare with a partner.

2moro.   Gr8   Thx   XLNT   ILY   RUOK

Excellent!   I love you.   Tomorrow.   Are you OK?   Thanks.   Great!

B Read the article. Find four reasons why text messaging can be useful.

C U L8R

If you're one of the 70% of cell-phone users who use text messaging, you know that **C U L8R** means "See you later." "Texting" is now *the* new way to talk (or "tlk"), especially for young people. But why is that?

It's a love thing.

There's no doubt about it, text messages are for personal communication. Only 10% of messages are work related, and the peak hours for texting are between 10:30 and 11:00 at night!

Most users (64%) say texting is a good way to send romantic messages — it's easier to say "I love you" in a text message than in a phone call. Maybe that explains why more people now use texting to send Valentine's Day messages.

ILY = I love you.

LUWA<3 = Love you with all my heart

Upsides and downsides

Generally, texting is cheaper than making phone calls. It's also more direct, since you can send or get information without having to ask and answer polite "How are you?" questions.

And it's more discreet, too. No one can hear your "conversations," and you can receive text messages almost anywhere — at work, in meetings, or in class. You can also use texting in noisy places like nightclubs, where using a cell phone is difficult.

A new language?

Because it's quicker to "write" without apostrophes and vowels, texting has its own language. And it's fun to use the symbols. There's a best-selling dictionary (or "DXNRE") for texting called *Wan2tlk?*

Some people say that texting encourages bad punctuation and spelling. On the other hand, more teens are writing than ever before. Now, that has to be a good thing!

:) = a smile

;) = I'm just kidding.

:-O = I'm surprised.

C Read the article again, and answer the questions. Then compare with a partner.

1. What do people use texting for?
2. Why does texting need its own language? How is it different from "real English"?
3. What are some of the advantages of text messaging?
4. Why do some people think text messaging is bad?

2 *Listening* Text messaging

Read the sentences below about text messaging. Then listen to Ally, and check (✓) the sentences she agrees with. Which ones do you agree with? Discuss with a partner.

☐ *It's convenient.*

☐ *It wastes time.*

☐ *It's fun.*

☐ *It's good for emergencies.*

☐ *It's less embarrassing than talking on the phone in public.*

☐ *It's annoying. It makes phones "beep" a lot.*

☐ *It's quicker than a phone call.*

☐ *It's difficult. The symbols are hard to learn.*

3 *Writing* The pros and cons

A *Pair work* Choose one of these ways of communicating. Make a list of its advantages and disadvantages.

e-mail   regular mail   instant messaging   text messaging

<u>Advantages of cell phones</u>
- Cell phones are useful.
- They're convenient.
- You can make calls from anywhere.

<u>Disadvantages of cell phones</u>
- They're annoying.
- They ring during concerts and movies.
- People talk in a loud voice.

B Now write a short article on your topic. Use your list and the help note below.

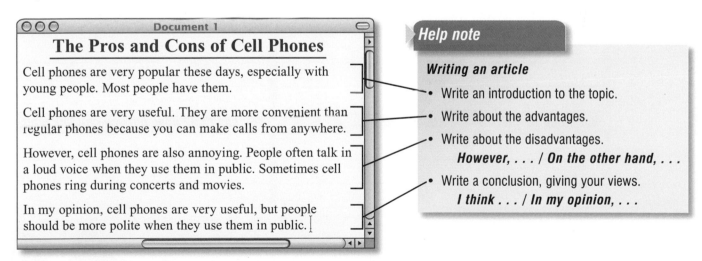

Document 1

The Pros and Cons of Cell Phones

Cell phones are very popular these days, especially with young people. Most people have them.

Cell phones are very useful. They are more convenient than regular phones because you can make calls from anywhere.

However, cell phones are also annoying. People often talk in a loud voice when they use them in public. Sometimes cell phones ring during concerts and movies.

In my opinion, cell phones are very useful, but people should be more polite when they use them in public.

Help note

Writing an article

- Write an introduction to the topic.
- Write about the advantages.
- Write about the disadvantages.
  However, . . . / On the other hand, . . .
- Write a conclusion, giving your views.
  I think . . . / In my opinion, . . .

C *Group work* Read your classmates' articles. Whose opinion do you agree with?

4 *Free talk* Which is better?

See *Free talk 10* for more speaking practice.

Vocabulary notebook

Phone talk

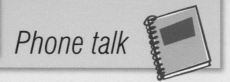

Learning tip *Learning expressions*

One way to learn expressions is to make a note of the situations when you can use them.

1 Match the expressions with the situations.

1. "I'm sorry. I have the wrong number." ____
2. "There's no answer." ____
3. "We have a bad connection." ____
4. "The line is busy." ____
5. "Where were we?" ____

a. You can't hear someone clearly.
b. You call the wrong number by mistake.
c. You come back to a conversation after an interruption
d. The phone rings and rings, but nobody answers it.
e. The person you are calling is talking on the phone.

2 What expressions can you use in these situations when you are on the phone? How many can you think of for each situation? Complete the chart.

You have problems getting hold of someone.	You ask to speak to someone.
You have problems with the call while you're talking.	**You say why you're calling.**
You ask if it's a good time to talk.	**You restart the conversation.**
You need to interrupt the conversation.	**You can't talk now, but you can talk later.**

On your own

Make a phrase book for different situations – for example, making calls. Carry it with you, and learn the phrases.

Appearances

In Unit 11, you learn how to . . .

- use *have* and *have got* to describe people.
- use phrases with verb + *-ing* and prepositions to identify people.
- talk about what people look like.
- show that you're trying to remember a word.
- use *You mean* to help someone remember something.

Jennifer   Donald   Andrea   John   Erica   Bruce

Before you begin . . .

Look at the picture. Can you find someone who . . .

- is short?
- is tall?
- is young?
- is old?
- is thin?
- is heavy?
- has long hair?
- has short hair?
- has dark hair?
- has blond hair?

Family traits

Alice   What does your twin sister look like, Heather? Do you look alike? I mean, are you identical twins?

Heather   No, we look totally different. Hayley's a lot taller than me. She takes after my dad.

Alice   How tall is she?

Heather   Six three.

Alice   Huh? . . . **How** tall is she?

Heather   Six foot three. I'm serious.

Alice   No kidding! So does she have curly black hair like you?

Heather   No, she's got straight blond hair and blue eyes. And she's thinner than me, too. I mean, she's really skinny.

Alice   She sounds like a model.

Heather   Actually, she **is** a model!

1 Getting started

A Listen. Alice and Heather are meeting Heather's sister at the airport. Can you find Heather's sister in the picture? Practice the conversation.

Figure
it out

B Can you make questions about Heather and Hayley for these answers? Then ask and answer with a partner.

❶ A _____ ?
   B No, they don't look alike.

❷ A _____ ?
   B Well, she's tall and thin.

❸ A _____ ?
   B She's six foot three.

2 Grammar *Describing people; have got*

What does Hayley look like? She's tall and thin.	Do Hayley and Heather look alike? No, they look totally different.	**have got = have** Who**'s got** curly hair? I do. I**'ve got** curly hair.
Who does she look like? She looks like her father.	What color is Hayley's hair? It's blond.	He**'s got** blond hair.
How tall is her father? He's six (foot) seven (inches tall). He's two meters five.	Does she have curly hair? No, she has straight hair. (No, she's got straight hair.)	*Who's got = Who has got* *I've got = I have got* *He's got = He has got*

About you → **Pair work** Discuss these questions. How much information can you give?

In conversation . . .

Don't confuse these questions:
What's she like? =
What kind of person is she?
What does she look like? =
Can you describe her?

1. How tall are you? Are you taller than the other people in your family?
2. What color are your eyes? What color is your hair?
3. Who do you take after in your family? How are you alike?
4. What does your teacher look like?
5. Who's got very short hair in your class? Does anyone have very long hair?
6. Does anyone in the class look like someone famous?
7. Are any of your friends over six feet tall? How tall is your best friend?
8. Do you know any twins? Do they look alike?

"How tall are you?" *"Five ten. I'm taller than my dad – he's five seven."*

3 Speaking naturally *Checking information*

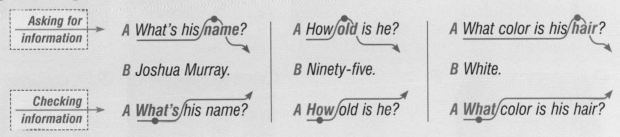

Asking for information	Checking information
A What's his name?	A What's his name?
B Joshua Murray.	A How old is he?
A How old is he?	A What color is his hair?
B Ninety-five.	
A What color is his hair?	
B White.	

A Listen and repeat the questions and answers above. Notice how the stress and intonation are different in the checking questions.

About you → **B Pair work** Ask your partner to describe his or her best friend.
Ask information questions and checking questions. Then change roles.

*A **So, tell me about your best friend. What's her name?***
*B **Her name's Sam.***
*A **What's her name?***
*B **Sam. It's short for Samantha.***
*A **How tall is she?***

1 Building vocabulary

A Listen and say the sentences. Check (✓) the features you like. Tell the class.

"I like mustaches."   *"I like muscular people."*

1

☐ He has **a beard** and **a mustache**.

2

☐ She has **pierced ears**.

3

☐ He has **a shaved head**. He's **bald**.

4

☐ She wears **braces**.

5

☐ She has **long fingernails**.

6

☐ He wears his hair in **a ponytail**.

7

☐ She's got **freckles** on her nose.

8

☐ She wears her hair in **cornrows**.

9

☐ She wears **glasses**.

10

☐ He's very **muscular**.

11

☐ She wears **braids**.

12

☐ He's got **spiked hair**.

Word sort → **B** For each feature, think of someone you know, and write a sentence. Then compare with a partner.

1. My boss has a beard and a mustache.
2. My mother has pierced ears.

2 *Building language*

A Listen. Find Rosa's roommate and Rosa's brother in the picture. Practice the conversation.

Jason So, is your new roommate here?

Rosa Yeah, she's right over there.

Jason Oh, which one is she?

Rosa She's the woman standing by the table.

Jason The one with short hair?

Rosa No, the woman with the ponytail.

Jason Oh, she looks nice. And who's that guy talking to her? He looks kind of weird.

Rosa You mean the guy in the yellow pants? That's my brother Jimmy.

Figure it out → **B** Can you complete these sentences about the picture?

1. Rosa's the woman _____ the curly hair.
2. Jason's the guy _____ next to Rosa.
3. Jimmy's the guy _____ the yellow pants.

3 *Grammar* *Phrases with verb + -ing and prepositions*

She's the woman **standing** by the table. **wearing** (the) black pants.	Which one is your roommate? The woman **with** the long hair.
She's the one **by** the table. **with** the long hair. **in** the black shirt.	Who's the guy **talking** to Rosa's roommate? **With** the yellow pants? That's her brother. Who's the guy **in** the blue shirt? Which one? The one **with** glasses? That's Jason.

A Look at the people on page 107, and cover their names. Match the questions and answers. Then ask and answer the questions with a partner.

1. Who's the tall man in the striped shirt? _____
2. Who's the woman standing next to Donald? _____
3. Who's the man in the suit? _____
4. Who's Erica? _____
5. Who's the muscular guy in the sweater? _____
6. Which one is Andrea? _____

a. She's the short one wearing the skirt.
b. With his hand in his pocket? That's John.
c. With the black pants? That's Donald.
d. Wearing jeans? That's Bruce.
e. The tall blond one? That's Jennifer.
f. The one with long hair talking to John.

About you → **B** *Pair work* Ask and answer questions about the people in your class.

"Who's the man in the blue shirt sitting next to Claudia?"   *"That's Marco."*

4 *Vocabulary notebook* *What do they look like?*

See page 116 for a useful way to log and learn vocabulary.

1 Conversation strategy *Trying to remember words*

A These people are trying to remember something. Can you match their questions with the responses?

1. "My teacher wears those tiny braids . . . what do you call them?"____
2. "I saw that British soccer star at a café today. Uh . . . what's his name?"____
3. "For tennis, do you wear a – what do you call it – around your head?"____

a. "David Beckham?"
b. "A sweatband?"
c. "Cornrows?"

Now listen. What does Lori tell Jin Ho about their old classmate?

Lori Do you remember that cool guy in our class last year? Oh, what's his name? You know . . . he always wore those baggy pants with all the pockets. What do you call them?

Jin Ho You mean cargo pants.

Lori Yeah. And he had long hair and a funny little beard . . . what do you call that?

Jin Ho Do you mean a goatee? . . . Oh, I know. You mean Max!

Lori That's right, Max. Well, don't look now, but he's sitting right behind you. And he's wearing a suit and tie and everything.

Jin Ho A suit and tie? No way!

Lori Yeah, and he's got short hair. He looks different!

Notice how Lori uses expressions like these when she can't remember a name or a word. Find examples in the conversation.

What's his / her name?
What do you call it / them?
What do you call that . . . / those . . . ?

B Complete the conversations with expressions like the ones above. Then practice with a partner.

1 A Do you remember when everyone wore those shoes – _____ – the ones with really thick soles?

B Oh, yeah. Platform shoes. I had some. They hurt my feet!

2 A Who was that musician, _____ ? With his hair in those long, twisted things, _____ ?

B Oh, dreadlocks? You mean Bob Marley.

3 A That's a really cool watch. Is it a – _____ – an underwater watch?

B Yeah. A diving watch.

SELF-STUDY
AUDIO CD
CD-ROM

2 *Strategy plus* You mean . . .

You can say **You mean . . .**
or ask **Do you mean . . . ?**
to check what someone is talking
about, or to suggest a word or name.

*Do you mean
a goatee? . . .
Oh, I know. You
mean Max.*

What words are these people trying to think of? Respond using *You mean . . .*
or *Do you mean . . . ?*

1. *A* I'm going to buy a pair of those baggy pants with lots of pockets.
   B   You mean cargo pants.

2. *A* My brother has long hair, and he wears it in a, um . . .
   B _____

3. *A* My friend has these cute little spots on her nose.
   B _____

4. *A* When I was a kid, I wore those things on my teeth.
   B _____

5. *A* What's the word to describe a person with no hair?
   B _____

6. *A* What do you call twins when they look exactly alike?
   B _____

3 *Listening and speaking* Celebrities

A Listen to Jan and Liz talk about photos of celebrities in a magazine. Who are
they talking about? Number the pictures.

Julia Roberts

Penélope Cruz

Lucy Liu

Cameron Diaz

Gwyneth Paltrow

Nicole Kidman

B *Pair work* Talk about celebrities but don't say their names. Before you begin,
make a list of names and things to say about each person. Can your partner guess who
you are talking about?

A I really like that movie director from Taipei. His movies are very different.
B Oh, do you mean Ang Lee? Yeah, I love his films.

How we looked

1 Reading

A Brainstorm! How many words about hair and hairstyles can you think of? Make a class list.

> spiked hair   bleached hair   bangs

B Read the article. Which hairstyles do you know about? Which do you like?

Hairstyles
through the
decades...

Do you know how people wore their hair 10, 20, or 30 years ago? Look back at the hairstyles of the last 50 years. There are some styles that come back again and again.

The 1950s were the beginning of the "rock 'n' roll" era. In the early '50s, men had short hair, but singer Elvis Presley changed all that when he combed his long hair into a "**pompadour**" and "**duck tail**." The ponytail was a popular hairstyle for young women.

The '60s was the decade of the Beatles, who caused a sensation when they grew their hair long – to their ears!

In the late '60s and the early '70s, the "**hippie look**" was in style. Men and women grew their hair very long, and many men wore beards. And the "**Afro**" was a popular hairstyle for African-Americans and anyone with curly hair or "**perms**."

The 1960s

Punk rockers shocked everyone with their multicolored, **spiky** hair in **the '70s**. Then in the late '70s and '80s, the soap opera stars made "**big hair**" popular – women wore their hair very long, curly, and full.

The 1950s

The "new romantic" women of **the '80s** wore hairstyles from the 19th century – **long curly** hair and **French braids**. For many men, the "**mullet**" cut (short on top and long in the back) was the hairstyle to have.

The 1970s

In **the '90s**, **dyed** hair became stylish. Both men and women started changing the color of their hair or adding highlights. Some men began to bleach their hair blond.

The 1980s   The 1990s

What will people say about the hairstyles of the early 21st century? Look around you. Do you see any styles that are really "new"?

C Read the article again. Are the sentences true or false? Correct the false sentences.

	True	False
1. Before Elvis Presley, guys wore their hair in a pompadour.	☐	☐
2. In the '60s, the Beatles had very short hair.	☐	☐
3. In the '70s, curly hair and long hair were fashionable.	☐	☐
4. Everybody wore French braids in the '80s.	☐	☐
5. In the '90s, more people started to change the color of their hair.	☐	☐
6. Musicians and singers started some of the fashions in the last 50 years.	☐	☐

2 *Listening* Next year's fashions

Listen to a fashion editor answer questions about the styles for next year. Complete the chart. Which ideas do you like? Discuss with a partner.

	For men	*For women*
1. general look		
2. clothes		
3. accessories		
4. hair		

3 *Writing and speaking* This year's "look"

A *Group work* Discuss the questions. Make notes of the different ideas.

1. What clothes are in fashion today?
2. What are the "trendy" hairstyles?
3. What makeup is everyone wearing?

4. What jewelry and accessories are popular?
5. What do you like about today's "look"? What don't you like?

B Write a fashion article describing the current "look." Use your notes.

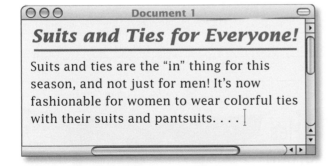

> ○○○ Document 1 ⊝
>
> ## Suits and Ties for Everyone!
>
> Suits and ties are the "in" thing for this season, and not just for men! It's now fashionable for women to wear colorful ties with their suits and pantsuits. . . . |

Help note

Describing new trends

Short hair is now **in style** or **fashionable**. Long hair is **out of style**. Glasses are becoming **popular**. **It's fashionable** for women to wear . . .

Less formal expressions

Short hair is **"in."** Long hair is **"out."** Tattoos are the **"in" thing** right now. They're very **trendy**.

4 *Free talk* What's different?

For more speaking practice, go to the back of the book.
Student A: See *Free talk 11A*. Student B: See *Free talk 11B*.

Learning tip *Writing true sentences*

Use your new vocabulary in true sentences about yourself or people you know.

1 What do these people look like? Match the sentences and the people.

1. He has short hair and green eyes. __d__
2. She has short hair. _____
3. He's bald and he wears glasses. _____
4. She's wearing earrings. _____
5. She wears her hair in braids. _____

6. He's short and a little heavy. _____
7. She has freckles. _____
8. She has long hair and big brown eyes. _____
9. He's tall and thin with blond hair. _____
10. She has curly hair. _____

2 Write three sentences about each of these people. What do they look like?

1. a family member _____
_____

2. a classmate _____
_____

3. a close friend _____
_____

4. yourself _____
_____

5. another person _____
_____

On your own

Look at three different people this week. You can be at home, in a store, on the bus, at a restaurant – anywhere. What do they look like? Think of how to describe them. Then write sentences.

He's green and bald and...

Looking ahead

In Unit 12, you learn how to . . .

- use *will*, *may*, and *might* to talk about the future.
- use *if* and *when* and the present tense to refer to the future.
- talk about plans and organizing events.
- use *will* to make offers and promises.
- say *All right* and *OK* to agree to do something.

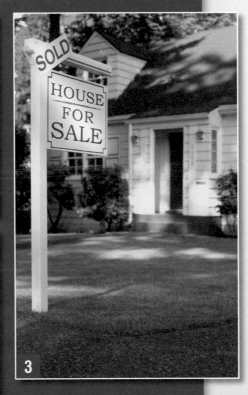

Before you begin . . .

Which of these things do you think you are going to do in the next five years? How sure are you? Absolutely sure? Pretty sure? Not at all sure?

- get a new job
- move to a new city
- buy your own place
- travel to another country

What are your plans for next year?

①

Christy Lewis

"Well, I'm graduating from college next June, so I guess I'll look for a job. I know it won't be easy to find one – so I may go on for a master's degree. We'll see."

②

Laura Chang

"I'm not sure. I might look for a better job. Before that, though, I'm going to ask my boss for a promotion. But I probably won't get one, so . . ."

③

Paul Reade

"Well, my friends are going to travel around Europe for two months. I hope I'll be able to go with them. But it'll be expensive, and I might not be able to afford it."

④

Jim and Katie Conley

"We're going to have a baby in March, so both of us will probably take some time off from work. I'm sure the baby will keep us both very busy."

⑤

Joe Etta

"I'm going to retire – I'll be 65 in June – and my wife's already retired. So we'll probably move to Florida in the fall, or maybe Arizona. We won't spend another winter here – that's for sure!"

1 Getting started

A 💿 Listen and read. Do you have the same plans as any of these people?

Figure it out

B Can you choose the correct words to make these sentences more accurate?

1. Christy **is going to / may** study for a master's degree.
2. Laura thinks **she'll probably / she probably won't** get a promotion.
3. Paul **might go / is going** to Europe with his friends.
4. Jim and Katie **are going to / might** have a baby.
5. Joe and his wife **will probably / are going to** move to Florida.

2 Grammar *Future with will, may, and might* 💿

You can use **will** to give facts or predictions about the future.	You can use **may** and **might** (or **will***) to show you are not 100% sure about the future.
It**'ll** be expensive to travel around Europe. The baby **will** keep us busy! I**'ll** be 65 in June. It **won't** be easy to find a job.	I **may** go on for a master's degree. I **might not** be able to afford it. We**'ll probably** take some time off from work. **Maybe** we**'ll** move to Arizona.
I'll = I will *won't* = will not	*Use **will** *with expressions like* **I guess**, **I think**, **maybe**, *and* **probably**.

Avoid will to talk about plans or decisions already made. Use the present continuous or going to.

I**'m going** to Europe next year. I**'m going to** visit Paris.   (NOT ~~I will go to Europe next year. I will visit Paris.~~)

About you ➤ Answer these questions about your future. Then discuss the questions in groups. Who has interesting plans for the future?

1. What are you going to do at the end of this course?
2. Are you going to look for a (new) job this year?
3. Are you going to study for a degree or certificate?
4. Do you have plans to move to a new apartment?
5. Do you think you'll be able to take a vacation next summer?
6. Are you going to travel abroad in the next couple of years?
7. Do you think you'll live in another country someday?
8. Do you think you'll ever be rich or famous? Why or why not?
9. What are your goals for the next five years?

A *What are you going to do at the end of this course?*
B *I'm going to take a vacation. I'm going to Australia!*
C *I'm not sure. I might look for a job.*
D *I guess I'll probably take another course.*

3 Speaking naturally *Reduction of will*

	your best friend **will** always be your friend?	(friend'll)
	the teacher **will** be a millionaire someday?	(teacher'll)
Do you think	your parents **will** ever move to another city?	(parents'll)
	all your friends **will** have children?	(friends'll)
	anyone in the class **will** be famous someday?	(class'll)

A 💿 Listen and repeat the questions above. Practice the reduction of *will* to *'ll*.

About you ➤ **B** *Pair work* Ask and answer the questions. Think of more questions to ask about the future.

A *Do you think your best friend will always be your friend?*
B *Yeah, I think he will. I think we'll always get along and . . .*

1 Building vocabulary

A 🔊 Listen and say the words. Do you know anyone with these jobs?
Do you know anyone who wants to have these jobs? Tell the class.

"My neighbor is a firefighter. He loves his job."   *"My cousin wants to be a dentist."*

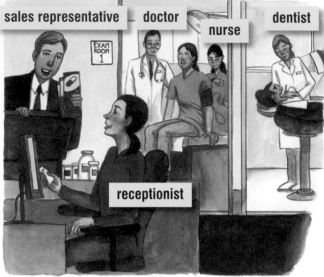

Word sort

B Complete the chart with jobs from above. Add ideas. Then compare with a partner.

Who . . .			
has an interesting job?	**has a rewarding job?**	**has a difficult job?**	**earns a lot of money?**
journalists			

" I think journalists have an interesting job. They travel a lot, and . . ."

2 Building language

A Listen. What is Beth's problem? Practice the conversation.

Andrew I can't believe we just have one more year of college!

   Beth I know.

Andrew What are you going to do when you graduate?

   Beth Well, I may go to law school if I get good grades next year.

Andrew Oh, I'm sure you will.

   Beth Well, you never know. My parents will be disappointed
if I don't go into law. They're both lawyers.

Andrew Wow. That's a lot of pressure.

   Beth Yeah. And after I graduate, I'll be able to work in their firm.

Andrew Uh-huh. Well, that's good.

   Beth Yeah, but I don't really want to be a lawyer. . . . I want to be a journalist.
I guess I need to decide before I go home for the summer.

Andrew Well, good luck!

> *Figure it out*

B *Pair work* Can you complete these sentences about Beth?

1. Beth may go to law school when she _____ from college – if she _____ good grades.
2. Beth needs to decide before she _____ home for the summer.

3 Grammar *Present tense verbs with future meaning*

In complex sentences about the future, use the simple present after if, when, after, and before.	What are you going to do **when you graduate**? **If I get** good grades, I may go to law school. My parents will be disappointed **if I don't go** into law. **After I graduate**, I'll be able to work in their firm. I need to decide **before I go** home for the summer.

A Choose the correct verbs, and then complete the sentences with your own ideas.

1. When class **is / will be** over today, I'm going to _____ .
2. Before **I go / I'll go** to bed tonight, I'll probably _____ .
3. Maybe I'll _____ next weekend if **I have / I'll have** time.
4. When my English **is / will be** totally fluent, I hope I'll be able to _____ .
5. If **I earn / I'll earn** a lot of money in the next ten years, I may _____ .
6. In the future, if I **don't / won't** have a good job, I might _____ .
7. I hope I'll be able to _____ after **I retire / I'll retire**.

> *About you*

B *Pair work* Compare your sentences with a partner.

A **When class is over today, I'm going to go shopping.**
B **Well, I think I'll just go home. I might pick up a movie on the way.**

4 Vocabulary notebook *Writers, actors, and artists*

See page 126 for a useful way to log and learn vocabulary.

1 Conversation strategy *Making offers and promises*

A Can you think of more offers you can make in this situation?

> A *Let's have dinner at my place. I'll order a pizza.*
> B *OK. I'll bring some soda.*
> C *And I'll _____ .*

Now listen. What does Eve offer to do? How about Mark?

Eve	*I'm really looking forward to the picnic tomorrow.*
Mark	*Me too. . . . Uh, do you want me to drive this time?*
Eve	*No, I'll drive. I won't drive too fast! I promise. I can't afford another speeding ticket.*
Mark	*All right. But will you remember to put gas in the car before we go?*
Eve	*Of course I will. We only ran out of gas that one time!*
Mark	*OK. So, I'll buy some sandwiches and potato salad and stuff. Could you bring your beach chairs?*
Eve	*All right. And . . . I'll bring my beach umbrella.*
Mark	*Great. And if you want, I'll call you in the morning and remind you about the gas.*

Notice how Eve and Mark use *I'll* and *I won't* to make offers and promises. Find examples in the conversation.

> *"I'll drive."* (an offer)
> *"I won't drive too fast."* (a promise)

B Two friends are planning a hiking trip in the mountains. Match one friend's comments with the other friend's promises and offers. Then practice with a partner.

1. How are we going to get there? I can't drive. _d_
2. Do we have to leave early? I might oversleep. _____
3. I'm not sure I have the right kind of boots. _____
4. Will you remember to bring a map this time? _____
5. Who's going to bring the food? _____
6. Are we going to hike all day? I'm not in shape. _____

a. I will. I'll make some chicken sandwiches.
b. Don't worry. I'll plan a short walk if you want.
c. Yes. I won't forget. I promise!
d. That's OK. I can. I'll borrow my parents' car.
e. I have an extra pair in your size. I'll bring them.
f. If you want, I'll call you when I wake up.

About you → **C Pair work** Plan a day trip with a partner. Make offers and promises. Use the ideas above.

"Why don't we go to the beach?"   *"OK. I'll drive, if you want."*

SELF-STUDY
AUDIO CD
CD-ROM

2 Strategy plus *All right and OK*

You can use *All right* or *OK* when you agree to something.

Could you bring your beach chairs?

All right.

OK.

▶ **In conversation . . .**

OK is about 6 times more frequent than *All right*.

OK

All right.

Respond to the questions with *All right* or *OK*, and make an offer with *I'll*. Then practice with a partner.

1. *A* Could you take a look at my computer today? I think it has a virus.

   B _____ .

2. *A* Can you call me sometime this weekend? I need to ask a favor.

   B _____ .

3. *A* I want to buy a digital camera. Can you help me choose one?

   B _____ .

4. *A* I'm going to paint my apartment next weekend. Could you help me?

   B _____ .

A **Could you take a look at my computer today?**
B **All right. I'll stop by your desk after lunch.**

3 Listening and speaking *Promises, promises*

A 💿 Listen to Mike and Jill organizing a class reunion. What does each of them say they'll do? Complete the sentences.

1. Jill says she'll _____ or _____ everyone.

2. She promises she'll remember to bring _____ .

3. She says she'll _____ online and pay _____ .

4. Mike says he'll _____ .

5. He says he'll try not to _____ .

6. He promises he won't forget to bring his _____ and his _____ .

B *Group work* Plan an end-of-the-year party or picnic for your class. Make a list of things to do, and decide who is going to do each thing on the list.

A **We should reserve a party room at a restaurant.**
B **OK, I'll call and do that. Which restaurant?**

In the future . . .

1 Reading

A Brainstorm! What will life be like in the future? Will it be better or worse for most people? Why? Tell the class.

"I think life will be better. People will be healthier, and we'll have better medicine."

B Read the article. Which predictions did you already know about? Which were new?

What will life be like in the future?

Body and health Health watchers predict that in many countries people will get taller. We will also get heavier. This is because we're eating more junk food and exercising less. However, we may not have to diet in the future. Scientists are working on a device to break down fat with ultrasound. Let's hope!

Online . . . all the time Before long, we'll all be on the Web – all the time. Everything around us, including clothes, jewelry, and even glasses, will contain devices that connect us to the Internet. For example, with tiny cameras in your sunglasses, you'll be able to take a picture – or a movie – and send it to a friend.

Automated homes The technology is already here, but by the 2030s most homes will be fully "automated." With computer chips in most appliances, you'll be able to turn on the heat or the lights just by making a phone call home. Scanners in your "smart" refrigerator will read the bar codes on food packages, and then tell you when the food goes bad. Even better, your refrigerator will go online to order more food when you run out. No more grocery shopping!

Work and play

In 20 to 30 years' time, only 20% of people will work in an office, and more of us will work from home.

But that doesn't mean we'll be able to watch TV all day. With videophones and webcams, the boss will be able to keep in touch and see exactly what we're doing. Uh-oh.

You may not have to commute to work, but if you want to drive on the weekend, you'll have to use a smaller, environmentally friendly car, reserve road space in advance, *and* pay road charges.

More brain power? Scientists say they'll be able to build a computer that is like a human brain by 2020. Robots with these artificial brains will do many jobs that humans do today. Road travel should become safer because cars will operate themselves. So by the 2030s, there won't be any more car accidents.

We'll be able to put computer chips in the human brain to make us smarter and increase our knowledge. But soon computers will become more intelligent than people. Some futurologists predict that by 2050, computers may even take control of our lives. Scary, huh?

C Read the article again. Check (✓) the predictions the article makes.

☐ 1. People will get taller, but they'll also be fatter.
☐ 2. People will probably use ultrasound to lose weight.
☐ 3. Everyday items will connect to the Internet.
☐ 4. Computers in our refrigerators will choose our food for us.
☐ 5. Fewer people will work in an office.
☐ 6. By 2030, there will be more car accidents.
☐ 7. Computers will become smarter than human beings.

D *Pair work* If the predictions are right, will they make our lives better or worse?
Discuss with a partner.

A *Our lives will be worse if we get fatter. We'll have more health problems.*
B *Yes, I agree. We'll need more doctors to take care of us.*

2 Listening and writing *I can't wait!*

A Listen to Sue and Bob discussing these predictions from the article.
For each one, who says it's a good idea? Check (✓) Sue or Bob.

Prediction	Who says it's a good idea?		Why is it a good idea?
	Sue	*Bob*	
1. a "smart" refrigerator	☐	☐	_____
2. a videophone	☐	☐	_____
3. a self-driving car	☐	☐	_____
4. a computer chip in the brain	☐	☐	_____

B Listen again. Write *one* reason why Sue or Bob thinks it's a good idea.
Do you agree? Discuss with a partner.

C Write a short article about one of the predictions. Will it make our lives better or worse?
Why? Give three or four reasons.

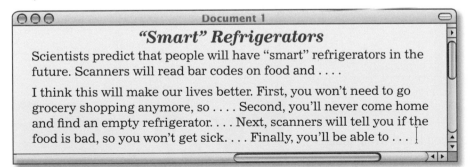

Document 1

"Smart" Refrigerators

Scientists predict that people will have "smart" refrigerators in the future. Scanners will read bar codes on food and . . . .

I think this will make our lives better. First, you won't need to go grocery shopping anymore, so . . . . Second, you'll never come home and find an empty refrigerator. . . . Next, scanners will tell you if the food is bad, so you won't get sick. . . . Finally, you'll be able to . . . |

▶ Help note

Listing ideas

First, you won't need to . . .
Second, you'll never . . .
Next, scanners will . . .
Finally, you'll be able to . . .

3 Free talk *I might do that.*

See *Free talk 12* for more speaking practice.

Vocabulary notebook

Writers, actors, and artists

Learning tip *Grouping vocabulary*

Write new vocabulary in groups. You can group words by their endings or by their meanings. You can group expressions by different topic areas.

Talk about jobs

The jobs people mention most in conversation are *lawyer*, *teacher*, and *doctor*.

1 Look at these jobs. Group them by their endings. How many other jobs can you add to each list?

✓actor	journalist	dentist	electrician	letter carrier	architect
artist	musician	writer	paramedic	travel agent	librarian
nurse	police officer	doctor	receptionist	firefighter	assistant

-er / -or	-ant / -ent	-ist	-ian	other
actor				

2 Think of expressions for these different topics, and add a topic of your own. How many expressions can you think of for each one?

Work	Home and family	Education	
get a promotion	have a baby	take an exam	

On your own

Make a list of 20 people you know. What jobs do they do? Write their jobs in English. How many new words do you learn?

126

1 Who's who?

A Complete these sentences about Jane and Sonia. Fill in sentences 1–4 with comparatives and sentences 5–6 with prepositions. Then compare with a partner.

1. Jane is _____shorter_____ and _____ than Sonia.
2. Sonia's hair is _____ and _____ than Jane's.
3. They've both got freckles, but Jane has _____ freckles.
4. Sonia is wearing _____ jewelry.
5. Jane's the one _____ the black T-shirt, and Sonia's the one _____ the yellow blouse.
6. Sonia's the one _____ the spiked hair, and Jane's the one _____ the ponytail.

B Can you write each sentence in another way?

> 1. Sonia is taller and heavier than Jane.

2 Can you guess what I mean?

A How many words and expressions can you add to the chart? Compare charts with a partner.

Describing faces	*Describing hairstyles*	*Ways of communicating*	*Jobs*
have freckles	have a ponytail	send a text message	electrician

B *Pair work* Student A: Explain a word or expression to a partner. Student B: Guess the word.

"You can do this with your telephone or computer."   *"Do you mean send a text message?"*

3 Can you complete this conversation?

Complete the conversation with the words and expressions in the box. Use capital letters where necessary. Practice with a partner. Then role-play the conversation, and use your own ideas.

I've got	what do you call it	all right	you mean	just	what was I saying	hold on a second	I'll
✓ this is	have a bad connection	wearing	let's see	with	where were we	I'll call you back	

Greg Greg Waters.

Kenji Hello, Greg. ____This is____ Kenji from the office in Tokyo. I was _____ calling to ask . . . What time are you arriving tomorrow?

Greg Well, I have my ticket here. _____ , I arrive at, um, 3:30.

Kenji OK, _____ come to the airport to meet you. Oh, _____ – I've got another call.

Greg _____ . . . .

Kenji Hi. Sorry about that. So, _____ ? Oh, yes, I'll meet you. So how will I recognize you?

Greg Well, I'm tall and _____ blond hair and –

Kenji Sorry, Greg, I can't hear you. It seems we _____ .

Greg OK. Listen, _____ . . . .

Kenji Hi. That's better. So, _____ ?

Greg I was describing myself. So, um, I'll be the blond guy _____ sunglasses, _____ a USA T-shirt.

Kenji Um, OK. Maybe I should wear a – _____ ? A thing with my name on it so you can find me?

Greg _____ a badge. Good idea!

4 Future plans and dreams

Circle the correct verb form, and then complete the sentences with true information. Tell your sentences to a partner.

1. When **I'll get / I get** home tonight, I'm going to _____ , and I might _____ , but I probably won't _____ .

2. If **you'll want / you want** help with your homework this weekend, **I'll help / I help** you. I'm not _____ on Saturday, but I may _____ on Sunday.

3. I promise **I'll buy / I buy** all my classmates dinner if **I'll win / I win** the lottery this year. I'll also _____ , and I might _____ , too.

4. If I ever **will become / become** famous, I **won't / don't** change. **I'll still be / I'm still** myself, and I won't _____ .

Self-check

How sure are you about these areas?
Circle the percentages.

grammar
20% 40% 60% 80% 100%
vocabulary
20% 40% 60% 80% 100%
conversation strategies
20% 40% 60% 80% 100%

. . . .

Study plan

What do you want to review?
Circle the lessons.

grammar
10A 10B 11A 11B 12A 12B
vocabulary
10A 10B 11A 11B 12A 12B
conversation strategies
10C 11C 12C

Free talk 1 Me too!

Class activity First write your answers to these questions. Then ask your classmates the questions. Find people who have things in common with you. Write their names.

	My answers	Classmates with the same answers
1. What's your favorite color?	blue	Kumiko
2. What food do you hate most?		
3. What sport do you play?		
4. How many sisters do you have?		
5. How many hours a week do you watch TV?		
6. What's your favorite day of the week?		
7. How often do you have dinner with your family?		
8. What do you usually wear on weekends?		
9. What time do you usually get up on Sundays?		

A **What's your favorite color, Kumiko?**
B **Blue. How about you?**
A **Me too. All my clothes are blue and . . .**

Free talk 2 The game of likes and dislikes

1 Think of one thing for each section of the chart. You have three minutes to write in your answers.

I enjoy watching _____ . (a sport)	**I can't play** _____ . (a sport)	**I'm good at** _____ . (an activity)
I think everybody loves _____ . (a type of music)	**I'd like to play the** _____ . (a musical instrument)	**I want to learn (to)** _____ . (a hobby)
I'm interested in reading about _____ . (a topic)	**I can't stand talking about** _____ . (a topic)	**I hate watching** _____ . (a type of TV show)

2 Group work Compare your charts. If anyone in the group has the same answer as you, score one point. Who scores the most points?

A **OK, I enjoy watching golf. How about you?**
B **I enjoy watching ice-skating.**
C **I do too! So we each get one point.**
D **I enjoy watching ice-skating, too, so I get a point, too!**

Score box:

A	B	C	D
	1	1	1

1 *Pair work* Read the questions and possible answers to your partner. Circle your partner's answers. Then change roles.

1. **How much exercise are you getting these days?**
  a. A lot. (4–6 hours a week)
  b. Some. (1–3 hours a week)
  c. None at all.

2. **What kinds of food do you generally eat?**
  a. A balanced diet with lots of fruit and vegetables.
  b. Some balanced meals and some fast food.
  c. Mostly snacks and fast food.

3. **How much sleep do you get?**
  a. Enough. (7–8 hours)
  b. Too much. (9–12 hours)
  c. Too little. (4–6 hours)

4. **How many hours do you work or study every week?**
  a. 30–40 hours.
  b. 40–50 hours.
  c. 50–60 hours.

5. **How much water do you drink?**
  a. 8 glasses a day.
  b. About 4 glasses a day.
  c. Very little.

6. **How often do you get headaches?**
  a. Never.
  b. Once or twice a month.
  c. Once a week.

7. **How often do you get a checkup?**
  a. Once a year.
  b. Once every 2–3 years.
  c. Never.

8. **What do you do when you are stressed?**
  a. I take a break and relax or exercise.
  b. I try not to worry about it.
  c. I don't do anything. I'm too busy.

9. **How often do you get colds?**
  a. Never.
  b. Sometimes.
  c. Often.

10. **If you are sick or overtired, do you . . .**
  a. take a day off, stay home, and relax?
  b. do your usual routine, but go to bed early?
  c. do your usual routine?

2 Figure out your partner's score. Give 3 points for each **(a)** answer, 2 points for each **(b)** answer, and 1 point for each **(c)** answer. Add them together for the total. Then read the health profile to your partner.

a	____ x 3 =	____
b	____ x 2 =	____
c	____ x 1 =	____
	= ____	*Total*

Health Profiles

24 to 30 points
You are taking very good care of your health. That's good news! If you have any **(b)** or **(c)** answers, then you can still improve. See if you can make one improvement each month.

17 to 23 points
You are taking pretty good care of your health, but you can do better. If you want to feel really good and have a lot of energy, choose two things to improve each month. You can do it!

10 to 16 points
You are not taking good care of your health. You need to change your diet and your lifestyle. Sleep and exercise are very important, and so is relaxation. Choose three things to improve each month and start today!

1 Group work Create a new special day or festival. You can use the ideas given or make up anything you want! Complete these sentences about your new event.

1. Our new festival or special day is called _____ . (*name*)
2. It's going to be on _____ . (*date*)
3. There's going to be _____ and _____ . (*events*)
4. Everyone is going to _____ . (*activity*)
5. Everyone is going to eat _____ . (*food*)
6. People are going to buy _____ . (*items*)
7. Nobody is going to _____ . (*activity*)
8. It's going to be _____ . (*"fun," "interesting," . . .*)

Grandma's Day

Chocolate Festival

No-Homework Day!

Get-Up-Late Week

National Skip-Class Day

2 Class activity Ask three classmates from other groups questions about their new festivals and special days. Take notes.

A **What's your new festival called?**
B **It's called "Laugh-a-Lot Day," and it's going to be on March 8th.**

3 Choose one festival that you'd like to celebrate. Tell the class why.

"I'd like to celebrate Laugh-a-Lot Day because people are going to tell jokes all day."

Pair work Student A: Read the brochure about Seasons Resort. Your partner has a brochure for Breezes Resort. Take turns asking questions. Do the resorts have the same attractions? Decide which resort you would like to go to.

"Is there a water park at Breezes Resort?"　　*"A water park? No, there isn't, but there's an . . ."*

It's **fun, fun,** *fun*
at **Seasons Resort!**

Sports:	**Splashaway Water Park** – Pools and water fun for the whole family!
	Crazy Golf – Miniature golf for all ages!
Dining:	Over 50 fast-food restaurants for eating out!
Shopping:	Outlet mall just 30 minutes away. Over 200 brand-name stores!
Movies:	3 multiplex cinemas with 20 screens. See all the latest movies!
Entertainment:	Nightly concerts. Top international bands!
	Fun Plaza – Video arcade, bowling, and disco roller-skating!
	Waxworks Museum – See your favorite celebrities!

Class activity Ask your classmates questions about their childhood. Write notes about each person.

Find someone who . . .	Name	Notes
1. was born at home.	_____	_____
2. didn't like playing outside.	_____	_____
3. wasn't good at music.	_____	_____
4. liked to play board games.	_____	_____
5. always had bruised knees.	_____	_____
6. was on a sports or an athletics team.	_____	_____
7. changed schools two or three times.	_____	_____
8. had a teddy bear.	_____	_____
9. got into trouble a lot.	_____	_____
10. liked to eat vegetables.	_____	_____

"Were you born at home?"   *"Did you like playing outside?"*

Pair work Student B: Read the brochure about Breezes Resort. Your partner has a brochure for Seasons Resort. Take turns asking questions. Do the resorts have the same attractions? Decide which resort you would like to go to.

"Are there any concerts at Seasons Resort?"   *"Let's see. Um, yes. There are . . ."*

Something for everyone at Breezes Resort!

Sports: Sports center with tennis, badminton, and racketball courts.

Olympic-size indoor and outdoor swimming pools.

Nine-hole public golf course. Open all year.

Dining: Fine dining at 15 international restaurants with world-famous chefs!

Shopping: European-style shopping street with designer boutiques and antiques.

Movies: Arts Cinema features foreign films in original versions with subtitles.

Entertainment: Free concerts daily in Breezes Garden – classical or jazz.

Sculpture Park with works from all around the world!

Summer Theater – see plays in the Breezes tent every evening!

Role play Look at the pictures. Imagine you and your friend are taking a vacation together. Choose a role (A or B), and take turns giving and responding to advice.

A *You should probably put your ticket in your pocket.*

B *Oh, OK. Good idea! Can you hold my coffee for me?*

A *Sure. And by the way, . . .*

Free talk 8   *All about home*

Group work Discuss the questions. How are you alike? How are you different? Does anyone have an unusual answer?

1. What's your favorite room at home? What do you like about it?
2. What's your favorite piece of furniture? Where did you get it?
3. Do you have a lot of plants in your home? How about pictures?
4. What's your kitchen like? Do you spend a lot of time in it?
5. Is there a lot of clutter in your bathroom? Whose is it?
6. What's in your bedroom? Is it neat or messy?
7. Does your family do a big "spring cleaning" every year? What do you do?
8. Is there a room you'd like to redecorate? What would you like to do?

Look at the picture. Bob just crashed into a lamppost. Try to remember as many details as you can. You have one minute. Then turn to *Free talk 9B* on page H.

Free talk 10   *Which is better?*

Pair work Choose three questions to discuss. Give reasons for your answers. Do you agree?

Is it better . . .

☐ 1. to have a digital camera or a regular camera?

☐ 2. to shop online or in a store?

☐ 3. to have a cell phone or a regular phone?

☐ 4. to leave a message with a person or on voice mail?

☐ 5. to use e-mail or text messaging with friends?

A Well, I think it's better to have a digital camera. It's more fun. You can see the pictures right away.

B Yeah, but I think you can take better pictures with a regular camera.

Free talk 11A   What's different?

Pair work   Student A: These people are at the mall on Saturday morning. Your partner has a picture of the same people on Saturday afternoon. In that picture, each person is different in one way. Ask questions to find out what's different. Where did each person go?

A **Do you see the woman with the dark hair?**
B **Yes. Is she wearing a green dress?**
A **Yes. So that's the same. Does she have a ponytail?**

B **No, she doesn't. Her hair is short.
   So that's the difference.**
A **I guess she went to the hairdresser.**

Free talk 12   I might do that.

Class activity   First answer the questions. Then interview two classmates, and write their answers. If you find out something interesting, continue the conversation.

Can you think of . . .	My answers	_____	_____
1. something you might do next year?			
2. something you'll probably never do in your life?			
3. something you think you'll do when you retire?			
4. something you'll definitely do if you earn a lot of money?			
5. a place you'll probably visit in the next five years?			
6. someone you'll probably see next week?			
7. something new you'd like to try?			
8. something you may do when you get home tonight?			

A **Can you think of something you might do next year?**
B **Well, actually, my family might move next summer.**
A **Really? To another city?**

1 Pair work How much can you remember from the picture in **Free talk 9A**? Discuss the questions below. Do you agree on the answers?

1. What was Bob doing when he crashed into the lamppost?
2. What else was he doing?
3. Was he wearing a helmet?
4. Was he wearing red sneakers?
5. What else was he wearing?
6. How many other people were in the picture?

7. What was the young boy holding?
8. What did the woman on the sidewalk shout?
9. Was she listening to music?
10. What color was the car?
11. Was the driver wearing sunglasses?
12. Can you remember any other details?

2 Now look at the picture in **Free talk 9A** again to check your answers. How many did you get right?

Free talk 11B   *What's different?*

Pair work Student B: These people are at the mall on Saturday afternoon. Your partner has a picture of the same people on Saturday morning. In that picture, each person is different in one way. Ask questions to find out what's different. Where did each person go?

A *Do you see the woman with the dark hair?*
B *Yes. Is she wearing a green dress?*
A *Yes. So that's the same. Does she have a ponytail?*

B *No, she doesn't. Her hair is short.*
   So that's the difference.
A *I guess she went to the hairdresser.*

Self-study listening

Unit 1

A *Track 1* Listen to the conversation on page 6. Eve and Chris are talking outside a club.

B *Track 2* Listen to the rest of their conversation. Choose the right answer. Circle *a* or *b*.

1. How long is Eve in New York?
   a. For the weekend.   b. For the week.

2. Who has two free tickets?
   a. Chris.   b. Eve.

3. Who are the tickets for?
   a. Eve and her brother.   b. Eve and her friend.

4. Where is Eve's friend from?
   a. New York City.   b. Miami.

5. Why is her friend in the coffee shop?
   a. He's cold.   b. He's hungry.

6. When Chris says, "Oh. OK," how does he feel?
   a. Happy.   b. Disappointed.

Unit 2

A *Track 3* Listen to the conversation on page 16. Matt and Sarah are talking about hobbies.

B *Track 4* Listen to the rest of their conversation.
Check (✓) true or false for each sentence.

	True	False
1. Matt likes to take photos of people.	☐	☐
2. Matt uses his computer to change his photos.	☐	☐
3. Sarah says Matt's photos look like paintings.	☐	☐
4. Sometimes Matt sells his photos.	☐	☐
5. Matt gives Sarah a photo of some teacups.	☐	☐
6. Sarah wants to make a sweater for Matt.	☐	☐

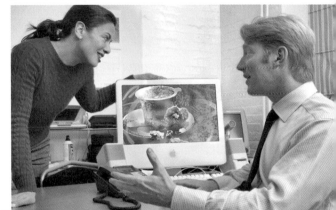

Unit 3

A *Track 5* Listen to the conversation on page 26. Adam and Yuki are talking in the library.

B *Track 6* Listen to the rest of their conversation. Make these sentences true
for Adam and Yuki. Circle the correct words.

1. Sometimes Adam **eats** / **sleeps** in the library during the day.
2. Adam puts his head on his **books** / **arms** and goes to sleep.
3. He usually sleeps for about **an hour** / **half an hour**.
4. **An alarm clock** / **A friend** wakes Adam up in time for class.
5. Adam's clock doesn't make any noise because **it's very small** / **it vibrates**.

Unit 4

A *Track 7* Listen to the conversation on page 38. Ray and Tina are talking about a festival.

B *Track 8* Listen to the rest of their conversation. Check (✓) true or false for each sentence.

	True	False
1. The festival has dance shows on two nights.	☐	☐
2. There are songs and dances from different parts of Mexico.	☐	☐
3. Tina wants to go to the festival on Sunday.	☐	☐
4. Tina and Ray decide to go to the dance show in the evening.	☐	☐
5. They decide to go to the children's parade in the morning.	☐	☐
6. Tina and Ray plan to wear costumes all afternoon.	☐	☐

Unit 5

A *Track 9* Listen to the conversation on page 48. Ben is telling Jessica a story.

B *Track 10* Listen to the rest of their conversation. Complete the sentences. Circle *a* or *b*.

1. Jessica lived _____ the school.
   a. down the street from
   b. an hour from

2. Jessica usually _____ home from school.
   a. walked
   b. took the bus

3. She wanted to ride the bus because _____ .
   a. she didn't like to walk
   b. her friends took the bus

4. The bus driver drove Jessica _____ .
   a. back to the school
   b. to her house

Unit 6

A *Track 11* Listen to the conversation on page 58. Kate is talking to the concierge at a hotel.

B *Track 12* Listen to the rest of their conversation. Choose the right answer. Circle *a* or *b*.

1. What is Kate's hobby?
   a. Fishing.   b. Scuba diving.

2. What does the aquarium have?
   a. A good restaurant.   b. A good gift shop.

3. Where is the aquarium?
   a. On First Avenue and River Street.
   b. On First Avenue by the river.

4. How long does it take to walk there?
   a. About forty-five minutes.
   b. About five minutes.

5. What does Kate decide to do?
   a. Swim in the pool.
   b. Read by the pool.

Unit 7

A *Track 13* Listen to the conversation on page 70. Chris and Adam are talking at work.

B *Track 14* Listen to the rest of their conversation. Complete the sentences. Circle *a* or *b*.

1. Chris and Adam want to do something _____ .
   a. tomorrow   b. next weekend

2. They plan to go _____ .
   a. camping   b. hiking

3. They plan to go on _____ night.
   a. Friday   b. Sunday

4. Adam says he has a tent and _____ .
   a. cooking things
   b. sleeping bags

5. The boss wants them to _____ .
   a. go back to work
   b. take a vacation

Unit 8

A *Track 15* Listen to the conversation on page 80. Jessica is arriving at Ben's apartment.

B *Track 16* Listen to the rest of their conversation. Who makes these requests? Check (✓) the name.

	Ben	Jessica
1. "Can you pass me the tissues?"	☐	☐
2. "Could you make the salad?"	☐	☐
3. "Would you mind watching the stove?"	☐	☐
4. "Can you get some peppers, too?"	☐	☐
5. "Do you mind if I get a drink of water?"	☐	☐
6. "Do you mind if I borrow your car?"	☐	☐

Unit 9

A *Track 17* Listen to the conversation on page 90. Matt and Emily are talking in Matt's kitchen.

B *Track 18* Listen to the rest of their conversation. Check (✓) true or false for each sentence.

	True	False
1. Emily was helping her mother cook dinner.	☐	☐
2. Matt likes Korean food.	☐	☐
3. Emily was making sweet rice cakes for dessert.	☐	☐
4. Emily served the rice cakes she made.	☐	☐
5. Emily's sister thought Emily made the rice cakes herself.	☐	☐
6. Emily told everyone the rice cakes were from the store.	☐	☐

Unit 10

A *Track 19* Listen to the conversation on page 102. Lucy and Maria are talking on the phone.

B *Track 20* Listen to the rest of their conversation. Complete the sentences. Circle *a* or *b*.

1. Lucy is _____ the first week of March.
   a. busy   b. free

2. Lucy says, "The weather there is a lot _____ it is here in March."
   a. cooler than   b. warmer than

3. Maria really wants to go to _____ .
   a. the beach   b. Mexico City

4. Maria wants to buy some Mexican _____ .
   a. pottery   b. jewelry

5. Maria says the pottery in Mexico is _____ .
   a. more expensive   b. less expensive

6. Maria tells Lucy that _____ all speak English.
   a. her cousins   b. her friends

Unit 11

A *Track 21* Listen to the conversation on page 112. Lori and Jin Ho are talking in a park.

B *Track 22* Listen to the rest of their conversation. Check (✓) true or false for each sentence.

	True	False
1. Max has to wear a suit for his job.	☐	☐
2. Max shaved off his moustache.	☐	☐
3. Mandy was in their Art History class.	☐	☐
4. Mandy is working in a bank now.	☐	☐
5. Jin Ho says, "Congratulations!" because Max got a job.	☐	☐

Unit 12

A *Track 23* Listen to the conversation on page 122. Eve and Mark are talking at school.

B *Track 24* Listen to their phone conversation the next day. Circle the correct words.

1. When the phone rings, Eve is **ready to leave** / **asleep**.
2. Eve **remembered** / **forgot** to get gas for her car.
3. Eve's beach chairs are in her **car** / **apartment**.
4. Eve needs to **take a shower** / **have breakfast** before she leaves.
5. Eve wants to have **breakfast** / **lunch** at Mark's place.
6. Eve decides to eat on the way to **Mark's place** / **the beach**.

SSL3

Unit 1

Chris So, your brother's in Miami 305? Who's your brother?
Eve This is him, right here.
Chris Wow. He's great. You know, I'm a really big fan. The band's from Miami, right?
Eve Yeah. How did you guess!
Chris So, are you from Miami, too?
Eve Yeah. I'm just in New York for the weekend.
Chris Really? Does your brother know you're here?
Eve Oh, sure. I have free tickets.
Chris Free tickets? That's great! Um . . . how many do you have? I mean, do you have an extra ticket?
Eve Actually, no. Sorry. I only have two – a ticket for me and a ticket for my friend.
Chris Your friend?
Eve Yeah, a friend from Miami. He's across the street in the coffee shop. It's too cold for him out here!
Chris Oh. OK.

Unit 2

Sarah Hey, Matt. Do you have time to show me your photos?
Matt Sure. Just give me a minute. . . .
Sarah So, what kind of photos do you take? Do you take pictures of people?
Matt Um, no, not really. I like to take pictures of things . . . you know, things around the house or outside.
Sarah Hmm. That's interesting.
Matt Yeah. Then I download them on my computer and change the colors and things like that. Look. These are pictures of some teacups.
Sarah Oh, wow. They're beautiful. Huh! They look like paintings! Do you ever sell them?
Matt Oh, no. They're not that good! But if you want, I can give you a photo for your office.
Sarah Really? I love this picture of the bicycles.
Matt Sure. I can frame it and everything.
Sarah Thanks, Matt. You know, maybe I can make you a sweater or something.
Matt Oh, I'd love that. Thanks.

Unit 3

Adam Well, I often take a nap during the day.
Yuki You do? Where?
Adam Uh . . . well, sometimes I sleep here in the library.
Yuki Right here? No way! How do you do that?
Adam Well, if I'm really tired, I find a quiet desk, and I just put my head on my books and go to sleep. . . .
Yuki Are you serious? How long do you sleep?
Adam Oh, usually for about an hour.
Yuki Do you wake up in time for class?
Adam Oh, yeah. I have an alarm clock.
Yuki An alarm clock? In the library? You're kidding!
Adam It doesn't ring. It vibrates, so it doesn't make any noise.
Yuki Oh, that's good. Um, anyway, can I ask you a question about our math homework?
Adam (yawns) Excuse me. Oh, sure.
Yuki Well, I don't really understand this one problem. . . . Where is it? . . . Oh, here it is. Yeah. Adam? Adam?

Unit 4

Ray Well, you know, there's dancing, too. . . . Spanish and Mexican dancing. They have special shows and everything.
Tina Oh, really? I love dance shows. When are they?
Ray Let's see. . . . They have shows on . . . Thursday, Friday, and Saturday nights. What do you think? Do you want to go?
Tina Um, maybe. What's in the show exactly?
Ray Well, . . . there's Spanish flamenco dancing. And songs and dances and things from different parts of Mexico.
Tina Huh. That sounds great. Um . . . OK. Let's go to the fiesta on Saturday. We can go to the music and dance show in the evening. . . .
Ray Yeah, let's do that. And we can see the children's parade in the morning.
Tina Right. And eat tacos and stuff all afternoon.

Unit 5

Jessica That's funny. You know, something similar happened to me.
Ben Really?
Jessica Yeah. Our house was right next to the school, I mean, right down the street, so I just had to walk a few minutes and I was home.
Ben Wow. My bus ride took an hour. You were lucky.
Jessica Yeah, but I always wanted to take the school bus. All my friends went home on the bus, and it looked kind of fun.
Ben Right.
Jessica So anyway, one day I just got on the bus with the other kids.
Ben You did?
Jessica Yeah. I don't know why. And we drove around, and all the other kids went home, and then the bus driver asked me, "Where do *you* live? Did I miss your stop?"
Ben How old were you?
Jessica Oh, six or seven. No, wait, maybe I was eight. Anyway, I said, "No. I live near the school." So he drove back.
Ben He drove you all the way back to the school?
Jessica Yeah. I was on the bus for hours. My mom was so worried.
Ben Oh, yeah.
Jessica She was really mad at me! But I just wanted to ride the bus.
Ben Oh, that's funny.

Unit 6

Kate So, what else is there to do? I mean, if I don't go to a movie.
Concierge Well, the aquarium is interesting. . . .
Kate Oh, did you say aquarium? I love looking at fish. My hobby is scuba diving.
Concierge Well, the aquarium's very nice. It has a good restaurant, too. It's on First Avenue and River Street.
Kate I'm sorry, it's where? First Avenue and . . . ?
Concierge First Avenue and River Street. It's on the corner. You can't miss it.
Kate Yeah. That sounds interesting. And it's within walking distance?
Concierge Well, yes, . . . if you like to walk.
Kate How long does it take to get there?
Concierge About 40 or 45 minutes.
Kate Oh, 45 minutes? Huh. . . . You know, I think I just want to sit by the pool and read. But thanks for your help!
Concierge You're welcome. Have a great afternoon!

Answer key
Unit 1 1. a   2. b   3. b   4. b   5. a   6. b
Unit 2 1. False   2. True   3. True   4. False   5. False   6. True
Unit 3 1. sleeps   2. books   3. an hour   4. An alarm clock   5. it vibrates

Unit 4 1. False   2. True   3. False   4. True   5. True   6. False
Unit 5 1. a   2. a   3. b   4. a
Unit 6 1. b   2. a   3. a   4. a   5. b

Unit 7

Chris Well, maybe we should do something next weekend.

Adam Yeah, that sounds OK. I'm not working next weekend.

Chris Oh, good. We could go camping or something.

Adam Yeah. We could take our mountain bikes.

Chris Great idea. We could go Friday and come back Sunday.

Adam Cool! Well, I have a tent and a couple of sleeping bags. . . .

Chris And I guess we should take some cooking things and flashlights and stuff. . . .

Adam And some warm clothes. It's going to be cold at night.

Chris Yeah, right. And we need food.

Adam Uh-huh. And . . . oh, no. There's the boss. . . .

Boss Hey, guys! You're not on vacation, you know.

Adam Um, sorry. . . . OK, well, let's talk later.

Chris OK. Back to work, I guess.

Boss Yeah! And by the way, I need you both to work next weekend. . . .

Chris/Adam Oh, no!

Unit 8

Jessica So, which knife should I use? This sharp one?

Ben Um . . . yeah, that's fine. Thanks. . . .

Jessica Oh, the onions! I'm crying! Can you pass me the tissues?

Ben OK. Here you go. That's funny. I never cry when I chop onions.

Jessica You don't? Oh, you're lucky. OK, so what else can I do?

Ben Well, uh . . . could you make the salad?

Jessica Sure. What do you have?

Ben Um, some tomatoes and some . . . oh, no, I forgot the lettuce. Listen, would you mind watching the stove while I run to the store?

Jessica No, not at all. Um, can you get some peppers, too?

Ben OK. Good idea.

Jessica Uh, do you mind if I get a drink of water or something?

Ben No. Go right ahead. There's some juice in the refrigerator.

Jessica Um, Ben, I don't see any juice. . . .

Ben Really? OK, so I need juice, lettuce, peppers, anything else? It's a good thing you came early, Jessica. Do you mind if I borrow your car?

Unit 9

Emily You know, I did something like that one time.

Matt Really? What happened?

Emily Well, I was helping my sister cook dinner for some friends. We were making Korean food.

Matt Yum! Korean food's great.

Emily Uh-huh. So, anyway, I was making sweet rice cakes for dessert. I was really happy because I was doing it myself, but it was a lot of work.

Matt Mmm. . . . I bet they were good.

Emily Well, . . . we were eating dinner and enjoying ourselves, and, um . . . I forgot about the rice cakes on the stove. When I went in the kitchen, they were ruined. I was so upset.

Matt I bet. So, what did you do?

Emily Well, just like you, I ran out to a store and bought some!

Matt You're kidding! Did anyone notice?

Emily No, no one did. And when I served them, my sister said, "These rice cakes are amazing! Emily made them herself." So anyway, I just smiled and didn't say anything.

Matt That's funny!

Unit 10

Maria I'm so glad you want to come. It's going to be great.

Lucy Oh, yeah. Mexico! I can't wait.

Maria Me neither. So, are you free the first week of March?

Lucy Yeah, that sounds good – the weather there is a lot warmer than it is here in March.

Maria Right. And we have to choose. . . . Oh, can you hold on a second? I have another call. . . . Sorry. Where was I?

Lucy We have to choose . . . ?

Maria Yeah, we can either go to the beach or to Mexico City. I really want to go to Mexico City. My cousins live there.

Lucy OK. Just think – we can eat Mexican food every day!

Maria Yeah. And I want to buy some Mexican pottery. It's a lot less expensive there.

Lucy Yeah, I bet. Oh, I'm so excited. Um, there's just one problem. . . . I don't speak Spanish.

Maria That's OK. I can speak for both of us! And don't worry – my cousins all speak English.

Unit 11

Lori Oh, no. He's coming over. Do you think he heard us?

Jin Ho I don't think so. We weren't talking very loud. Hi, . . . Max?

Max Hey, Jin Ho. Hi, Lori. How are you doing?

Lori Great.

Jin Ho Good to see you. You look really different!

Max Oh, yeah, the suit! Well, I work in a bank now, so I have to look professional. I shaved off my beard, too.

Lori And your hair is short. I almost didn't recognize you!

Max Well, life is different now. Say, do you remember Mandy . . . from Music History class?

Jin Ho Mandy . . . you mean the one with the spiked hair.

Lori Yeah. And her hair was orange, sometimes purple. . . .

Jin Ho Yeah. What's she doing now?

Max Teaching music. We, um . . . we got married last summer.

Jin Ho You did? Congratulations!

Lori That's great! So, Mandy's a teacher, huh? No more purple hair for her, I guess.

Max Right!

Unit 12

Eve Hello?

Mark Eve, hi! It's me, Mark. Um, did I wake you up?

Eve Oh, Mark, hi! No, I'm awake! Um, how are you?

Mark I'm good. So, are you ready?

Eve Ready?

Mark Yeah. Ready to leave for the picnic?

Eve Oh, right. Um, yeah, . . . almost.

Mark Great! Did you remember to get gas?

Eve (yawns) Uh, no. I'll get some before I come to your place.

Mark OK. And you got the beach chairs and umbrella, right?

Eve Yeah, they're here. I just have to put them in the car.

Mark So what time will you be here? Are you ready to leave?

Eve Well, almost. I just need to take a shower, and . . .

Mark Oh. Well, don't be too long!

Eve No, I won't. And when I get to your place, maybe we'll have time for breakfast?

Mark Breakfast? But it'll almost be time for lunch!

Eve Oh, good. Then I can eat a sandwich on the way to the beach.

Mark A sandwich? Oh, no, the sandwiches! I forgot.

Answer key

Unit 7 1. b   2. a   3. a   4. b   5. a

Unit 8 1. Jessica   2. Ben   3. Ben   4. Jessica   5. Jessica   6. Ben

Unit 9 1. False   2. True   3. True   4. False   5. True   6. False

Unit 10 1. b   2. b   3. b   4. a   5. b   6. a

Unit 11 1. True   2. False   3. False   4. False   5. False

Unit 12 1. asleep   2. forgot   3. apartment   4. take a shower   5. breakfast   6. the beach